Like There's
No Tomorrow

Like There's No Tomorrow

Meditations
for Women Leaving Patriarchy

Carolyn Gage

Common Courage Press   Monroe, Maine

Library of Congress Cataloging-in-Publication Data
Gage, Carolyn
Like there's no tomorrow: meditations for women leaving
patriarchy
Carolyn Gage.
p. cm.
Includes index.
ISBN 1-56751-105-8 (cloth). -- ISBN 1-56751-104-X (pbk.)
1. Feminism—Miscellanea. 2. Lesbian feminism—
Miscellanea. 3. Women—Psychology—Miscellanea.
I. Title
HQ1233.G34   1997
305.42-dc21   96-48436
CIP

Common Courage Press
Box 702
Monroe, ME 04951

207-525-0900   fax: 207-525-3068

First Printing

Contents

Introduction

"She declares that before her escape from slavery, she used to dream of flying over fields and towns, and rivers and mountains, looking down upon them 'like a bird,' and reaching at last a great fence or sometimes a river, over which she would try to fly, 'but it 'peared like I wouldn't hab de strength, and jes as I was sinkin' down, dere would be ladies all drest in white ober dere, and dey would put out dere arms and pull me 'cross.'"

—from an article about Harriet Tubman in
The Boston Commonwealth, 1863.

Harriet Tubman was the ultimate activist. She not only liberated herself, but she returned again and again to lead others out of oppression. When the War Between the States erupted, she returned again, this time to fight alongside the Union troops, liberating even greater numbers of enslaved people.

Harriet Tubman's activism was fired by a radical and visionary spiritual sense, as suggested by the newspaper article excerpted above.

History does not tell us the identity of these "ladies all drest in white," but Harriet was of Ashanti ancestry, and it would not be unreasonable to speculate that these were the spirits of her African foremothers—spirits of other women who had rebelled against their chains. Were these the women who threw themselves from the ships during the horrendous Middle Passage? Were they the women who fought back, who killed their would-be rapists and enslavers, who sabotaged equipment and destroyed the stolen property of their captors, who would not forget who they were and where they came from? Were these the women, like Harriet's mother, who cherished their daughters in defiance of a system that would reduce African American females to sexual commodities and chattel? Whoever these purported "ladies all drest in white" were, Harriet's vision of them provides a key to understanding what might otherwise

've been monumental foolhardiness or unprece-
fortune.

ere is a division between women who are political
activists and women who are proponents of the personal
growth, women's spirituality, and recovery movements. This
division is not an accident. It is the kind of split that is fundamental to patriarchy. As long as women believe activism will
render us martyrs or that focusing on our inner life requires
political apathy, we will remain a subject people.

Today, women desperately need to change the things we
have been taught to believe we cannot change. We stand at that
impasse with increasing despair, depression, suicidality, numbing. An increasing number of women are sinking with fatigue,
as Harriet did in her vision. And there are also large numbers
of women turning back to their chains, trading the harrowing
struggle with the uncertain outcome for a familiar oppression.

Is there a third choice for women? Is there a way to find
inspiration, rejuvenation, exhilaration in the struggle? Can we
experience serenity, sobriety, sanity from the heart of an activist
campaign?

I believe that we can. I passionately believe that each
woman can change the odds for herself through acquiring a
radical vision.

And Harriet's vision was not a passive one. She did not
wait for miracles when faced with challenges. She did not abandon common sense. She drugged the babies and she carried a
gun. Harriet's "ladies" did not spare her the challenges of a
physical disability, the struggle against poverty, or the many
close calls she experienced on her trips north. But Harriet held a
firm conviction that the rightness of her actions entitled her to
practical spiritual aid and comfort, and that conviction was realized in the success of her missions.

This is a meditation book for vision-building.

It is a book for the activist who is on the verge of a burnout,
who is appalled to discover in herself the makings of a tyrant—
or even a fascist—as she goes about the business of revolution.
This is for the woman noticing the widening split between the

needs of the movement and the needs of her own body, between her ideals and her practice, between her commitment to Women and her commitments to individual women, including herself.

It is also a book for our sisters in recovery for whom "one day at a time" may have been just a little too little, a little too late. This book is for my sister whose heart is broken—who has stopped trying because it's too exhausting, stopped dreaming, because it's too painful. It is a cruel taunt to ask this woman to accept the things she cannot change, because nothing less than a vision of full liberation can rouse the shattered in spirit.

This book is peopled with the spirits of many women— some of them living, some dead—but all of them warriors. Some are well-known in patriarchal culture, others well-known to women in minority communities, and some are my personal friends. Many are Lesbian-feminists.

These are women whose words and whose examples have pulled me over the line many, many times. These women have taught me to cultivate my anger, to mind other people's business when that business is the business of oppressing others, to hold on and hold out instead of letting go. These women have taught me to overturn instead of turn it over, and they have taught me, above all, to live like there's no tomorrow.

Carolyn Gage

Fighting

"I found that it is always better to fight than not to fight, always no matter what."

—Andrea Dworkin

These are the words of Andrea Dworkin, the courageous feminist philosopher, activist, and author who has fought so many long and frequently lonely battles against prostitution and pornography.

Fighting does not necessarily mean being out of control, losing, counter-attacking, or giving energy to a hopeless cause. In the martial art of Aikido, women learn to "get off the line"—to move to the side, out of line of the attacker, and to use the attacker's own momentum to throw him off balance. Just because one is being attacked does not mean that the attacker will have control over the speed, direction, or outcome of the interaction.

In patriarchy, fighting has been made to seem very disempowering to women—disruptive and sidetracking at best and suicidal at worst. In fact, fighting can be invigorating, a strengthening and stretching exercise. Fighting, like Aikido, can be practiced as a spiritual discipline, and one that integrates mind, body, and soul.

And, just as fighting back has been characterized as an undesirable option, so capitulation has been disguised to look like some kind of victory. Failure to confront or to defend oneself can be called "picking one's battles," "taking care of oneself," or "accepting the things I cannot change." The woman who fails to stand up for herself may justify herself by saying that she is choosing to "rise above it," choosing to "not take the bait," or choosing to "detach." She may, in fact, be fragmenting, numbing out, or practicing denial. These may be so second nature to her that she is not even aware that she is reinforcing her own toxic conditioning.

The doctrine of "choosing one's battles" is a dangerous one for the radical feminist. There is no form of collaboration, no matter how heinous, that cannot come under that banner. Fighting back is often the way to give the least energy to a situation.

Understanding and Vulnerability

—————➤●◄—————

"The greatest understanding is also the most vulnerable."
—Sor Juana Inés de la Cruz

Why is this? Because understanding is bedrock. Understanding can't be edited. Opinions, attitudes, perceptions, ideas, analyses, points of view—these are all fluid, subject to revision, open to debate. These can be adapted to the occasion, altered to fit the circumstances.

But understanding is not negotiable. It is a pure resonance with what is. Understanding is experienced not just in the head, in the imagination, in the logic. Understanding is received in the gut. Understanding is a homecoming; understanding is integration. And because of this, understanding is inflexible.

The woman who drifts through life on the currents of popular thought does not face resistance for the direction she travels. And if, in going with the flow, she finds herself pitched over the edge, she does not have to question whether or not her choices precipitated the calamity. The fall is experienced as inevitable, a change in the geography of the stream bed.

The experience of the woman who has achieved a measure of understanding is very different. She is, in the words of Sor Juana, "vulnerable." Because the nature of understanding is recognition, not interpretation, she can no more choose her experience than the mirror can choose what it reflects. She loses the ability to be polite, politic, or even tolerant. She becomes uncompromising, not as a stance, but because certain truths have become merged with her identity. She becomes incapable of divorcing actions and ideas from the context in which they are generated. She watches herself "sabotage" social interactions and career opportunities. If she does not voluntarily become more selective about her associates, she will find that such selectivity will be imposed on her by an almost ritualized shunning within her community.

Understanding may be arrived at accidentally. The scholar may achieve it in the course of her studies. The artist may achieve it in her search for an aesthetic. The lover may come to it in her attempts to give pleasure to her partner. And because understanding can arrive unbidden, the vulnerability that accompanies it can be terrifying. The woman who has always prided herself on her adaptability, on her survival skills, on her ability to "pass" in any environment, may find herself out of work, homeless, alone, impoverished. She may become agoraphobic, or she may self-identify as "crazy" in the mistaken belief that pathologizing herself will give her more control. Still identified with mainstream values, she may embrace a role as heretic or martyr, because, self-destructive as these roles are, they still offer the comfort of being rooted in the definitions of the culture. Being martyred is still some way of belonging. The key is to find or found a new society.

Sor Juana Inés de la Cruz, the seventeenth-century Mexican nun, was a brilliant writer and a Lesbian. Living in a culture where marriage was mandatory for women and education exclusive to men, she understood her vulnerability and took refuge in the separatist life of the convent.

Telling the Truth

———⟫●⟪———

"I had crossed the line, I was *free*, but there was no one to welcome me to the land of freedom.
I was a stranger in a strange land."

—Harriet Tubman

We've all read the fairy tales: Telling the truth results in rewards, medals of honor, parades, statues, promotion, gratitude from the whole village...

But life is not a fairy tale. In real life, the truth-teller will be ignored, and if that doesn't work, she will be discredited. When that fails, she will be shunned by family, friends, and community. If this period of grinding isolation does not cause her to recant, she can expect continued loss of opportunities for work, recreation, social contact, and artistic expression.

If she can hang in there long enough for the world to realize the rightness of her position, she can expect that someone else will "discover" the truth for which she has paid in blood. And that someone will probably not be as honest or as intrepid as the pioneer truth-teller, which will be precisely the reason she has been chosen as the designated discoverer and proprietor of the new idea. After a short period of time, it will be generally accepted that everyone always knew the truth anyway.

This is a discouraging scenario for one who is expecting to be treated like a heroine. But it is important for us to know what kind of reception we can expect for blowing the whistle, for standing up for ourselves, for naming our abuse, for describing our reality.

We can expect to be, like Harriet, "strangers in a strange land." But, also like Harriet, there will be those few who have tracked our exodus from patriarchy, and who are themselves preparing to escape. In time, we will have the privileged company of those women who are willing to put everything on the line for freedom.

And that is enough.

Acceleration

"My mother taught me that the gas pedal will get me out of more trouble than the brake."

—attributed to Lyn St. James

Not surprisingly, Lyn became a race car driver.

Why is her mother's advice sound? Because if one is really traveling, acceleration is less likely to cause a loss of control than sudden braking.

In life, many women have been taught to instinctively retreat at the first signs of danger. Danger seems to be an omen that we have been going too far or too fast, or both. This is logical, because in patriarchy women are not supposed to have any momentum or goals whatsoever—except those we have internalized from men.

Historically, the woman who wanted things: education, control over her sexuality, freedom from motherhood, a political life, her own career, rights to her own children, dress reform, and so forth, was accused of witchcraft, was fired, shunned, ridiculed, ex-communicated, divorced, incarcerated, drugged, lobotomized, raped, battered, and/or killed. We have a deep race memory of what happens to uppity women—that is, the women caught speeding.

But, as Z Budapest, Lesbian witch and founder of the Women's Spirituality Movement, reminds us: "The witch trials are over." We must challenge that instinctual fear. It is a new day for women. We can come out of our cells now. This is not to say that men are not still dangerous, but it is to say that there are enough of us now so that we are able to challenge the old taboos successfully. More and more of us are doing it every day. And as more and more of us do it, more and more barriers for women are falling.

If a lifetime of retreat and withdrawal have resulted only in poor self-esteem and depression, maybe it's time to put the pedal to the metal in our lives. What if, the next time we are given a reprimand for some form of uppityness, we counter with an action twice as uppity? And if we are having poor luck in meeting some goal of ours—what if we try setting one twice as high?

Remember, when the first "horseless carriages" came out, people were terrified by the new-fangled contraptions, tearing recklessly around at twenty miles an hour!

Holding Out

⟶⟶◆◄⟵

"I did not accept the job."

—Belva Lockwood

How often the world insists on the necessity of compromise! How compelling the arguments! And what incredible faith it takes to turn down the invitations to little death that are continually presented to us as "expedient measures." Small wonder so many women wake up at middle age to a life they never would have chosen as girls.

In traditional 12-step programs, there is a prayer that asks for courage to change what one can, serenity to accept what one can't change, and the wisdom to know the difference. In theory, a powerful spiritual discipline. In practice, often a dangerous trap.

This is because women have been overwhelmingly brainwashed to believe that we have no ability to change anything, except our own perceptions. This prayer can be used as a rationale for quitting, for retreating, for adjusting to abusive conditions, for living ever more constricted lives, and for being at peace with choices that should rankle us daily to the marrow of our souls.

Belva Lockwood was a teacher. She was offered a job at half the pay a male teacher would receive, which was the universal practice of her day.* She didn't accept the job.

Her refusal was a radical act when teaching was the best job around, when *no* teaching jobs for women paid any better. But in refusing the job, Belva made a commitment to herself to undertake a quest for a job commensurate with her self-esteem. She refused to allow the patriarchy to split her self-worth from her career goals. She would not collude in her own devaluation.

In not taking the job, Belva created a vacuum, and Nature, which, of course, is female, abhors a vacuum. This is a great secret for us radicals. But creating a vacuum is difficult, because it often looks like quitting or getting fired or failing or self-sabotaging or acting like you're better than everybody else. (Imagine how the teachers who accepted the job felt toward Belva!) Few women can stand the existential terror of hanging with a vacuum long enough to see another order brought into being, but for those who can stare down their demons— "Failure is impossible." (Susan B. Anthony)

And what came of Belva's vacuum? She went on to attend college. She became one of the first women attorneys, and she was the first woman to practice law before the Supreme Court.

Oh, yes, in 1884 she ran for President of the United States as the candidate for the Equal Rights Party. Unfortunately, women were not allowed to vote.

* Women have progressed since Belva's day. We are now paid well over 60% of men's wages.

Torture

"There's a part of me that says, I don't want to go
further with my creativity, because if people envy me,
they'll torture me. It's not so much a sense of
not being able to handle anything; it's a sense of not
being able to handle torture."

—bell hooks

These are the words of bell hooks, African American feminist and author.

And, yes, patriarchy loves to throw terms like "self-sabotage" and "women's fear of failure" at us. But when
almost any woman who achieves any power is at risk of
being tokenized, or at risk of being perceived as a token,
these terms are more of blaming the victim.

I was grateful to bell hooks for applying the term "torture" to the behaviors of envious people. These behaviors
can be very subtle, even though their effect is not.
Envious people just don't extend. Envious people say
things behind your back, ignore your work, pretend they
don't recognize you or the value of your work or the
extent of your struggle. Envious people are polite. They
may even offer token and crazy-making support in areas
that are not important, while they are sabotaging or withholding in the areas that are critical to your welfare.
Envious people will never admit they are envious, and
truly, many of them probably don't experience themselves that way. They genuinely believe that the object of
their envy is uppity, usurping, betraying, whoring, or
fraudulent. How do I know? Because I have been envious

15

and not admitted it to myself. And I have been an object of envy.

I think of a science fiction analogy for much of what happens to women: We are stalked and attacked by an invisible assailant. And as we roll around on the floor, choking, flailing, struggling to free ourselves—we look for all the world like we are just having some kind of fit. The kindest thing that might be said is that we are laboring under some genuine mental disability. The unkindest interpretation is that we are staging the event to attract attention.

Torture. That is the word. And the puzzled concern of bystanders or the sadistic withholding of women who have known the same stalking and struggle—these also are torture.

I stopped myself because of torture. I was touring nationally and running a theatre company. I did not have a good understanding of boundaries, and I was clueless about how to enforce them. I was being tortured beyond what I could bear, but because I could not see my attackers and because I could not name what I was experiencing, my body stopped me. I became too ill to perform or direct. And it took me years to figure out what was happening and why. And it took even more years to know what to do about it.

Torture is a good word. And so is envy. I encourage radical women to look for opportunities to use these words, because we have such strong natural resistance when it comes to confronting one another. Torture. Yes. Excellent word.

Freedom

"As I become freer, the need to show the world becomes greater."

—Bonnie Martinez

Bonnie Martinez is a visual artist whose work is, in her words, "solid visual, irrefutable screaming proof of the incest."

There is a common myth that recovery from trauma will allow the survivor to get on with "normal life," so that we can become the women we were before the rape—or the women we would have become if the incest had not occurred. Sentiments like that expressed in Bonnie's quotation are seen as dangerously retrogressive—that is, reflecting an unhealthy obsession with the perpetrator that will keep the survivor locked in a victim mode.

But are the choices revenge or forgiveness? Is the issue even justice?

Lesbian philosopher Mary Daly points out that the concept of justice as a "commodity long overdue," one that requires perpetual struggle, is hardly enough to fire the imaginations of women. In her words, justice "does not convey the object of this striving as *something that women create*."

So is there another option?

Mary Daly suggests that there is, and she calls it "nemesis." Her definition of nemesis is "virtue beyond justice, acquired by Inspired Acts of Righteous Fury." In a passage from *Pure Lust*, Mary describes nemesis as *"rewarding* power." This is a key distinction for survivors.

We must take hold of the transformational aspects of what we have been through. We will never be who we were before. We can never go back and re-experience our development free from the trauma. But we can embrace our difference and reap the rewards of our enhanced self-awareness, perceptions, networking, or activism. And much of this is achieved by showing the world our truth.

Bonnie's work is creative, expressive, and powerful. She collected several of her smaller drawings of incest and abuse—all from the child's point of view—and mounted them in a traditional family photo album, specifically to highlight the hypocrisy and the horror behind the myth of the patriarchal happy family. Mary Daly's alternate definition of nemesis reads "Virtue enabling Seers to unblindfold captive Justice," and this—not revenge—is a far more apt description of Bonnie's work and her mission.

Loss

—————◆—————

"I closed my eyes and tried to reach the pleasure I had known before but in vain. It was as if I could no longer recall the exact spot from which it used to arise, or as though a part of me, of my being, was gone and would never return."

"My whole body shuddered with a far away yet familiar pleasure arising from some unknown source, from some indefinable spot outside my being. And yet I could feel it somewhere in my body, a gentle pulsation beginning like a tender pleasure, and ending like a tender pain. Something I tried to hold on to, but to touch if only for a moment, but it slipped away from me like the air, like an illusion, or a dream that floats away and is lost. I wept in my sleep as though it was something I was losing now; a loss I was experiencing for the first time, and not something I had lost a long time ago."

"I held her eyes in mine, took her hand in mine. The feeling of our hands touching was strange, sudden. It was a feeling that made my body tremble with a deep distant pleasure, more distant than the age of my remembered life, deeper than the consciousness I had carried with me throughout. I could feel it somewhere, like a part of my being which had been born with me when I was born, but had not grown with me when I had grown, like a part of my being that I had once known, but left behind when I was born. A cloudy awareness of something that could have been, and yet was never lived."

— Nawal El Saadawi

These are passages from Nawal El Saadawi's novel, *Woman at Point Zero*. The novel, a sweeping indictment of Egyptian society, is the story of Firdaus, a woman imprisoned and awaiting execution for the "crime" of murdering her pimp.

Firdaus is a woman who has had her clitoris excised by her mother in the monstrous practice of female genital mutilation that was an accepted part of her culture. In the novel, Nawal describes the loss she experiences from the mutilation of her site of pleasure.

How can we live with the losses we have experienced? The loss of our bodies, of our sexuality, of our autonomy, of our creativity, of our capacity to trust, of our freedom, of our courage?

Woman at Point Zero is all about the meaning of loss. And in the heroine's quest for a life of dignity, she redeems these losses by her ruthless refusal to live in denial. She arrives at a sense of herself at "point zero," at a place "left behind when I was born." As Firdaus says at the end of her ordeal, "They do not fear my knife. It is my truth which frightens them. This fearful truth gives me great strength. It protects me from fearing death, or life, or hunger, or nakedness, or destruction. It is this fearful truth which prevents me from fearing the brutality of rulers and policemen. I spit with ease on their lying faces and words, on their lying newspapers."

Six years after the publication of *Woman at Point Zero*, Nawal El Saadawi found herself arrested as a political prisoner, and the courage she had projected in the character of Firdaus became manifest as her own.

Ridicule

"We shall enjoy it
As for him who finds
fault, may silliness
and sorrow take him!"

—Sappho (translated by Mary Barnard)

Who owns the power to ridicule—and by what virtue? Generally speaking, the dominant culture (and members thereof) own the power to ridicule—whether this culture arises in a corporate environment, or one determined by national media, or a culture evolved in a classroom of fourteen-year old girls. The dominance may be established through sheer numbers, or ownership, or management, or by what may be perceived as membership in a socially elite group.

The power to ridicule is not to be taken lightly. It aims directly for our self-esteem. I think of the courageous pioneers of dress reform who walked down the streets in their bloomer outfits, followed by jeering men and boys who threw manure on them. I think of the African American girls, with rotten tomatoes and eggs thrown at them, who walked into class for their first day in an all-white school.

Shaming and humiliating are potent strategies, because they bypass reason and ethics, appealing directly to our survival instincts as social beings. It is a knee-jerk response to shun someone who has separated herself from the herd—especially if the herd has become a pack and turned on her.

21

Fortunately, we are not creatures of instinct. We have the ability to critique a dynamic and, if we are practiced warriors, we have the ability to create our own contexts.

I remember the extreme poverty and amateurism of my first Lesbian theatre company. My productions would have been easy targets for ridicule by my professional peers. Many of the shows looked worse than the most amateur high school productions.

To survive, I reminded myself and my company of the reasons why we had no resources and very little experience, why mainstream audiences shunned us—even though our art spoke courageously of conditions for all women, not just for those of us who identified ourselves as Lesbians. I reminded myself that we would be arrested, executed, or "disappeared" for doing these plays in most countries in the world. I saw my theatre as a band of outlaws, exiles, political prisoners, warriors. Fighting shame was a daily discipline during those years.

I like this fragment of Sappho's, because it indicates that she knew the sting of ridicule and also the need to formulate a counter-strategy. With characteristic Lesbian moxie, Sappho appropriated for herself and her lovers the power to ridicule her ridiculers.

Wonder Women

———————

"If you ever
again tell me
how strong I am
I'll lay down on the ground & moan so you'll see
at last my human weakness like your own..."

—Chrystos

This is from "I Am Not Your Princess," a fierce protest poem against cultural appropriation of First Nations culture, and in this poem, First Nation poet and activist Chrystos names the subtle and confusing practice of marginalizing an activist in the name of valorizing her.

Just who are these "wonder women?" Are they women with nerves of steel, iron constitutions? Are they martyrs—as someone once accused Barbara Deming of being? Are they masochists who enjoy their pain?

Are they women with accidental integrity, women who somehow managed to slip through the socialization cracks? Or fragmented women who have painstakingly welded their broken parts together again, and the weld is now stronger than the original bonding?

What makes a woman risk her security, her pride, her identity? What makes a woman face her worst fears and go through them?

As Chrystos points out, these "wonder women" may be as weak and frightened, as vulnerable as any one of us. When we look at them and think, "Well, that was very brave, but *I* could never do something like that," aren't we actually dehumanizing these women in order to pro-

23

tect ourselves? And isn't that just exactly the way discrimination and prejudice always work?

Buckets

"What's the point of praying for rain, if you haven't got any buckets?"

—overheard at a women's music festival

The speaker was not really talking about rain. She was talking about social change. And she pointed out that people don't make revolutions; revolutions happen. This is not to say they come out of the blue. But they occur when the readiness for change creates the conditions to precipitate that change.

What are our buckets as radical feminists? What are the forms that might contain our bounty?

Well, for instance, what are these institutions we would be setting up if we had enlightened government-spending policies? What is the curriculum we would teach in a perfect world? What would our child-raising practices be if the welfare of the child was considered a priority in all areas of our life? What would our sexual practices be if we found ourselves suddenly showered with the qualities we lost through childhood terrorism and patriarchal brainwashing? How would we structure our day in a world where we could be sustained by what had meaning for us? How would we treat one another in a world where every woman was allowed to own her power?

You would be surprised how energizing, how radicalizing, and how *satisfying* it can be to get those buckets ready in the middle of a drought. And buckets—even empty ones—change the landscape. They do. They set everyone to thinking. And maybe, just maybe, sitting around with all those sturdy buckets to inspire us, we'll realize that it might not take a miracle from the sky after all, but just some powerful, get-down brainstorming and coalition to figure out some other way to get those buckets filled.

Identity

> "I did not use paint. I made myself up morally."
>
> —Eleanora Duse

Eleanora Duse was able to project the varying ages and conditions of her characters through her acting. She did not need to paint her face.

She saw make-up as a mask that would restrict her range of expression. Many actors perceive it as an enhancement, a visual aid in creating the illusion of the character they are playing.

But Duse was not interested in "playing characters." Her art was the art of transforming herself into the character. She did not need to look like the character. Because she *was* the character, the character would look like her.

How many of us are trying to fill someone else's shoes in our lives? How many of us are trying to be someone we're not? Even radical feminists are not exempt. Many of us have tried to adopt the clothing, the postures, the artistic styles, the organizations of the women we admire.

And this is natural. This is how we learn. We try on different roles, different costumes at various times in our lives. And I'm sure Eleanora started out with imitations and impersonations.

But at some point, she decided to dispense with the make-up. She decided to make whatever role she was playing completely her own. She no longer drew a distinction between her real face and her character's face. She would not allow herself to be ruled by the conventions of theatre, by the pressure of her peers, or by the expectations of the audience. She assumed the power to define her relationship to the work, and in doing so, she radically redefined the art of acting.

Where her contemporary, Sarah Bernhardt, was a genius at presentational acting styles, reveling in turgid love scenes and agonizing deathbed soliloquys, Eleanora Duse was natural and honest in her acting, foregoing sensational effects in her faith that nothing was more powerful or resonant than the simple truth.

Manipulating people and moving people are two different and mutually exclusive propositions. And they come from two very different starting places. The manipulator references to the audience: "How will this look? How am I doing?" The mover references to herself: "Do I really believe what I'm doing? How do I feel about myself?"

It takes an actor anywhere between ten minutes and two hours to apply make-up for a performance. On the other hand, it can take a lifetime to absorb all the nuances of a character.

Jobs

"I worked for one old woman when I was still a girl
for twenty-two years. Twenty-two years! And one day
at the end of them twenty-two, I went up to her and
asked if she could see her way clear to pay me a little
more. She'd like to had a heart attack right on the
spot! *Twenty-two years*, mind you. Had practically
raised her children for her, and all I was askin' was a
dollar and a half more, and she had the gall to stand
there and look at me like I had hit her with something. She come drawing herself up to me in a state of
clear shock and telling me... "Why *Lee-na*! I never
thought to hear *you-ou* talk as if you thought of this as
a *job*! ... Why, we ain't never thought of you as nothing other than just another part of our family!"

—Lorraine Hansberry

This is a quotation from Lorraine's screenplay of *Raisin in
the Sun*, a screenplay, by the way, that was never filmed.
It makes fascinating reading, especially when compared
with the version (not hers) that was eventually filmed.
The differences, not surprisingly, are political and about
racism and classism. Lorraine was polite about the
Hollywood version, but—especially since she had written such a radical screenplay—the differences must have
eaten at her.

But, back to the quotation. This is, of course, a reference
to the permutation of slavery euphemistically called
"domestic service." The double standard is that the
African American woman is expected to supply the emotional investment of a mother toward her employer's

children, but in return she is neither given a reciprocal emotional investment nor the financial support and security that a wife and mother of a middle class family could expect in return. She is paid the barest minimum wage—no retirement, no pension, no health insurance—with which she must provide for her own family. If she attempts to invest the job with the kind of minimum effort that minimum wages warrant, however, she is accused of being mercenary! What a patriarchal reversal!

"Company loyalty" is a similar ploy for exploiting women. I can remember a chain store where I worked as a salesclerk. There was a big inspection day, where our store would be in competition with the others in the chain. We were expected to come in *without pay* and clean the store! I also remember a convalescent home, where the staff nurses were expected to donate a half hour of work a week, because the home was affiliated with a church! At a restaurant where I worked, the waitresses were expected to punch out on the time clock and *then* go back and set up the station for the next waitress.

What's going on? Are we stupid? No, we are survivors. And survivors are often subject to syndromes we don't understand. One of them is called "displaced affect." Here's how it works: The victim becomes morally hyper-vigilant in an attempt to compensate for the excesses of her abuser. For example, the victim of a batterer may feel she is being abusive in expressing anger or even defending herself from attack. The victim of financial abuse may become recklessly inattentive to her own financial welfare, fearing that any concern for money makes her a scrooge. Exploited women workers, fearing charges of being mercenary, can often be bullied into donating their work or foregoing raises.

Survivors of abuse *must* have outside input in order to develop a healthy perspective. That, in a nutshell, is the beauty of a union.

Romantic Love Revisited

———⟫✦⟪———

"What led to my loving him for so long... was a feverish irritation which took possession of my faculties as a result of never achieving personal satisfaction."

—George Sand

Love is a funny word. I have found "respect" more useful. "Love" can refer to so many different and opposing states that is almost useless in terms of a meaningful referent.

In her science fiction novel *Native Tongue*, author Suzette Haden Elgin invented a language for women called "Láaden," and in it, she broke down the experience of "love" into specific categories:

áayáa—mysterious love, not yet known to be welcome or unwelcome

áazh—love for one sexually desired at one time, but not now

ab—love for one liked but not respected

ad—love for one respected but not liked

am—love for one related by blood

ashon—love for one not related by blood, but kin of the heart

aye—love that is unwelcome and a burden

azh—love for one sexually desired now

éeme—love for one neither liked nor respected

oham—love for that which is holy

sham—love for the child of one's body, presupposing neither liking nor respect nor their absence

Having only the word "love" to describe these many states, we end up brainwashing ourselves. We may feel that as long as we "love" someone, we can't leave them. We may feel a responsibility to care deeply for someone, just because we're being sexual with them at this time. We may feel absolutely crazy, because of addictive attraction toward someone who represents the antithesis of all our values. And, as the quotation by George Sand so eloquently illustrates, we may confuse the projection of our frustrated need for validation with love.

The next time you say or think the word "love," ask yourself to be more specific. You might be surprised.

Shooting the Deserters

———⟫•◦⟫⟫•◦⟫———

There is no quotation for this entry, but it is in commemoration of Harriet Tubman, the most famous conductor on the Underground Railroad.

Most people are aware that Harriet led hundreds of African Americans to freedom without ever "losing a passenger." One of the reasons for this is that she made it very clear that she would shoot anyone who tried to turn back.

Shooting the deserters was a harsh policy, but the deserters would have put the entire party in jeopardy. Also, their notions about being able to sneak back without being caught, or even of being dealt with leniently because they came back, were most likely unrealistic. But fear plays strange tricks on us, and the chains of our slavery can sometimes seem preferable to the terrors of the unknown.

Tubman was no doubt familiar with this syndrome. She had probably experienced it herself. One of the most difficult aspects of leaving an oppressive, but familiar environment is the torment of doubting oneself. In some ways, Tubman's policy relieved her passengers of this temptation: Turning back would not be an option, no matter how scary things looked. Knowing this, the passengers were compelled to handle their fears—or at least contain them—and to focus on the strategies that would enable them to get to Canada.

What about women leaving patriarchy? Aren't there days when it feels like it would have been easier/safer/healthier/more rewarding/more considerate to have stayed in the prescribed roles that serve the fathers? Or maybe there are just pieces of us who would like to sneak back—and maybe just for a visit. I am thinking of situations where it might appear to be to our advantage to pull rank on another woman by exploiting our classist, racist, ageist, ableist privelege. Or perhaps we are tempted to fall back on our ability to numb out in the old patriarchal way, because to speak up might cause trouble.

How many of us have been with a lover and felt the backward tug of patriarchal judgments or criticisms toward our partner? Do we have any idea what harboring these little deserters costs us in terms of progress toward liberation in our relationships? Do we realize they put the whole party in jeopardy?

A woman who commits to leaving patriarchy should take stock of just how dangerous and how significant that journey is going to be. It might not be a bad idea to sit down with all her different parts and explain the necessity for a "shoot-the-deserters" policy.

[Footnote: The "unsinkable" Molly Brown was said to have taken charge of one of the lifeboats of the *Titanic*, enforcing discipline with a gun taped to her wrist!]

Selective Identities

———————————

"When we spoke out as feminists, the Left as well as the Right accused us of importing foreign ideas, strange ideas that were popular among women in the so-called developed countries. You'd hear this sort of thing from anyone, from a Catholic who based his ideas on someone like St. Augustine — hardly a native son! — to a Marxist whose ideology came from just as far afield. I used to tell them: "Look, Lenin wasn't born here... neither did the Pope grow up in my neighborhood! Your political theory or your religious ideas are as foreign as my feminism is."

—Magaly Pineda

Born in the Dominican Republic, Magaly attended college in Puerto Rico, and then returned to Santo Domingo where she became involved with the Federation of Dominican Women, whose motto was "Shoulder to Shoulder with Our Men." Later in 1973, she organized Women's Promotion, which had a more blatant feminist agenda.

At this time, Magaly was drawing on the analysis of middle-class white feminists in the United States, and she began to realize that their situations were not analogous to the conditions for women in the Dominican Republic. For one thing, domestic service was so poorly paid in her country that even a woman with lower middle class income could afford one or two women working in her home. The pressures of working the "second shift" at home, which was radicalizing the middle class in the United States, was simply not a factor for the women Magaly knew.

She began to formulate her ideas for a "popularly-based feminism," and in 1980 she founded the Centro de Investigación Para la Acción Femenina (CIPAF) with a Chilean woman and a Puerto Rican woman. One of their first goals was to research issues of domestic and sexual violence. Later, CIPAF also did studies on abortion, prostitution, rural women, and women working in the free trade zones.

CIPAF's studies helped get women's issues onto the social agenda of politicians, but they also produced materials the organization could give back to the women, allowing them to become subjects in their own consciousness-raising.

Feminism has often been identified as a movement for and by white middle-class women in the United States. Charges of "cultural imperialism" have been leveled at women attempting to spread feminist ideology in other countries. And it is true, the women's movement in the '70s was contaminated by institutionalized racism, classism, homophobia, and colonialism.

But feminism does not "belong" to any group. It is a liberation movement, and different cultures — and different individuals — will apply their understanding of this ideology differently according to each one's process. Because of this, it is important for women to listen to one another and to learn. The principles of feminism, taken to their logical conclusion, call for the end of all oppression, and sooner or later we will all get there.

Mothers

⟫◦⟪

"The doctors told me I would never walk, but my mother told me I would, so I believed my mother."
— attributed to Wilma Rudolph

Thus spake Wilma Rudolph, childhood polio victim and adult Olympic track star. Obviously, Wilma's mother loved her. Wilma's mother looked at her daughter and saw beyond who she seemed to be, into who she could become.

But not all of us had mothers like Wilma's. For some of us, it was our mothers who were telling us we would never walk—even when we didn't have polio!

Women not only have the right to choose our mothers, but it is imperative that we do so. If our birth mothers fail to live up to the standard of support we equate with the word "mother," we need to be able to confront that fact and move on to finding the women who can meet our needs.

If we are protecting a toxic mother, we will have a hard time containing the radiation. Like a decimal in the wrong place, a corrupt ideal of mothering will skew all of our subsequent equations for love, for relations between women, for family, for self-confidence. Even if our mother died decades ago, even though we may appear to have broken out of the family mold with a fantastic career, an adoring partner, and so forth—trust me, nothing will move the decimal, except moving the decimal. Sooner or later there will be a day of reckoning, and days of reckoning have a way of hitting you when you're already down.

38

(Actually, every day is a day of reckoning, but when we are hale and hardy and practicing denial, we have the ability to table the agenda.)

Demoting a birth mother is not an easy task. It can feel like a merciless act of abandonment against an unfortunate woman, who was herself a victim of ___ (fill in the blank with "incest," "alcoholic parents," "battering," etcetera) It can feel like a supreme act of betrayal, of horizontal hostility. It can also feel like poor coping skills, so-called black-and-white thinking, or immature blaming of others for the problems in our own lives.

It may feel like maturity to "rise above" her continual petty assaults on our self-esteem. It may even seem radical to see past all of her damaged conditioning into the woman she might have been. Oh, be careful! What one is actually doing is ignoring that marvelous child-self inside all of us who is registering every put-down, every criticism, every insult. The adult sense of well-being one can get from "co-ing" a toxic mother is nothing more than the great relief to be siding with the perpetrator instead of the victim. When we cease to be bothered by a toxic mother, we are in the greatest peril of all.

What about choosing another mother? No, no one will love us unconditionally as adults and wait on us hand and foot. But healthy adult women can offer genuine caring, respectful modes of interaction, genuine understanding of our passions and points of view. They can be whole enough to be sincerely thrilled by our victories and honestly sympathetic about our defeats.

The world is full of healthy women, but we will never find them until we learn to pass on the unhealthy ones.

Art

"Like any artist with no art form, she became dangerous."

—Toni Morrison

This quotation refers to Sula, the heroine of Toni Morrison's novel by the same name:

"In a way, her strangeness, her naivete, her craving for the other half of her equation was the consequence of an idle imagination. Had she paints, or clay, or knew the discipline of the dance, or strings; had she anything to engage her tremendous curiosity and her gift for metaphor, she might have exchanged the restlessness and preoccupation with whim for an activity that provided her with all she yearned for."

For thirty years, visual artist Elizabeth Layton suffered from severe depression and episodes that are characterized in patriarchy as "mental illness." In the late fifties, she endured thirteen sessions of electroshock torture, euphemistically called "treatments." Drugs and therapy failed to "cure" her.

Then, at the age of sixty-eight, she took a class in contour drawing through a community recreation program. She discovered that she was an artist—and a powerful one.

Elizabeth's work is almost exclusively self-portraiture. She draws herself as Carrie Nation, Lady MacBeth, Eve, the Mona Lisa, Raggedy Ann. Her drawings are filled with symbols. Seeing an exhibit of her drawings, I was so overwhelmed by the compression of themes, the juxtaposition of personal and political iconography, the emotional intensity of the collection, that I needed to come back several times in order to assimilate the impact of the work.

As soon as she began to express herself with her art, Elizabeth's symptoms of "mental illness" vanished. Is it possible that there are some of us whose experiences of the world are too large to be contained by the ordinary channels of life? Is it possible that some of us have a capacity for integration, multi-dimensionality, and metaphoric construction that make us "crazy" unless we are given an outlet as boundless and as personal as our visions?

And is it possible that we were once all artists, before the brutally constrictive conditioning of childhood was imposed on us?

Is it sane to be crazy? Are those of us who are "differently minded" actually the saner, because we still feel the sensations of our patriarchally amputated fourth dimensional faculties?

And what would happen if every disturbed little girl, every "depressed" woman, was presumed by society to be an artist who had not discovered her art? Imagine the so-called mental patient being offered access to a smorgasbord of artistic disciplines, where she is mentored, nurtured, encouraged to express herself—to tell her most radical truth, with no taboos, no inhibitions, no judgments, and where the results of her efforts are taken seriously, given thoughtful feedback, and showcased for the benefit of others.

Success

➤━●━◆━

"You never conquer a mountain.
You stand on the summit a few moments,
Then the wind blows your footprints away."

—Arlene Blum

In 1978, Arlene Blum led the American Women's Himalayan Expedition on their climb of Annapurna. Witnessing an avalanche that came close to killing several members of the party, she experienced a radical shift in her priorities, putting the safety of the expedition ahead of any notions of personal glory. She was not a member of the summit teams, and she learned hard lessons on leadership when she made the unusual, but democratic decision to allow a second team to make a bid for the summit the day after the first team had already reached the top. This second team lost a support person at the last minute, and they never reached the top. It was three days before the bodies were located.

Victory is a slippery concept, and success can be as traumatic as failure. Material configurations are inadequate to satisfy the cravings of the human spirit. And standing on the summit means there's nowhere to go except down.

For the radical feminist, it may seem to be a cruel joke to discuss how to deal with success or recognition, since we are so seldom granted either. But remember, we are attempting summits where the air is exceptionally thin, where forward movement at all is unprecedented. Taking responsibility for our definitions of success and recognition is paramount, if we are to keep going. When we set our sights on a modest goal, one that would be easily attainable for men, with their hired sherpas and corporate equipment, and then fail to reach it, we place ourselves directly in the path of an avalanche of rage and/or self-contempt.

As radical feminists, it is critical that we continue to aim for nothing less than the most radical goal we can cherish. We can know that every base camp we establish without class systems, without authoritarianism, without sponsorship by institutions that oppress women is a miracle, regardless of the altitude. But we must never participate in our own demoralization by settling for less than that which inspires us with all our heart.

But in focusing on our summit, we need to be careful that we are not substituting symbol for substance, investing a material arrangement with the power that already belongs to us. Our foremothers fell into this trap by focusing on the achievement of suffrage as an ultimate goal. Voting is the act of making marks on a piece of paper. Although women's suffrage represented the *potential* for radical change, it was not synonymous with it. In fact, after women "won" the vote, the women's movement lost much of its impetus for fifty years, as the much-dreaded "women's party" failed to materialize and neither women candidates nor women's issues made significant gains. We are only now beginning to grapple with the brainwashing and internalized oppression that have prevented women from exploiting what power there is in the ballot.

Too often radical activists become over-burdened with strategies of resistance and survival. It can be a radical act to incorporate considerations of victory into our everyday thinking.

Impossibility

"I am a candidate for the Presidency of the United States. I make that statement proudly in the full knowledge that, as a black person and as a female person, I do not have a chance of actually gaining that office in this election year."

—Shirley Chisholm

Shirley Chisholm's example gave everyone pause. The racists and the woman-haters could snicker. The non-racist feminists and the non-sexist African Americans could stand up and cheer. And others could puzzle over why she did it. Who throws herself heart and soul into a lost cause?

But it wasn't a lost cause, and that is a crucial point to understand. Chisholm's goal was not to win, but to run, and to run as best she could. And she turned her liability into an asset, by making the very impossibility of her election into an election issue. Shirley Chisholm was presidential material and she knew it. Nothing demonstrated this more than her decision to run. She chose to conduct herself as if she were living in a right world. And whenever a woman does this, it catalyzes everything and everyone around us.

Chisholm's autobiography makes fascinating reading, and her entry into the world of Washington politics was a baptism of fire. Like Rosa Parks, Chisholm knew she was not going to get to the end of the line. But she put herself where she belonged. She refused to participate in her own marginalization. She made the racists and the woman-haters stand up and be counted.

It takes great courage to do this. And it also takes courage to stand with an ostensible loser. How many women reformers have felt the almost unbearable sting of being deserted by other women—even opposed by them, and sometimes by the very ones who would stand to benefit the most from our actions?

I remember founding my theatre company in a small town with a large professional Shakespeare theatre. I was sure that the women from this company, fed up with small and stereotyped roles that portrayed women as obstacles or rewards for men, would flock to moonlight in my theatre, where the plays were of, for, about, and serving the interests of women. What a shock, what a painful awakening, to realize that these actors would not even *attend* my plays—that they joined in ridiculing my efforts because of the scarcity of my resources!

Women like Chisholm are beacons to women like myself, and maybe someday my light will be a guide for another woman. We must remember and remind ourselves that men control the board. We must not be afraid of "losing" on their terms. *And we must not allow our hearts to be broken by the women who abandon us.* That is why I am writing this book—to create another tool whereby radical women can keep our focus on those whose lives can give us support and strength. Shirley Chisholm was a bright, bright light.

Promotion

"Wherever Minnie Fiske sits, *that's* the head of the
table."

—Remark about Minnie Maddern Fiske

Minnie Fiske was an actor in the last century who refused
to cater to a theatre that perpetuated sexist stereotypes
about women—and she refused to cater to the men who
promoted that kind of theatre. At the height of her career,
the Theatre Syndicate held a virtual monopoly on professional theatres in the United States. They controlled not
only all the New York theatres, but also the regional theatres on the touring circuits. The Syndicate was concerned with box office, not art, and they specialized in
"star-making" and brainless girlie-shows.

Minnie Fiske, who was performing Ibsen's plays and her
own adaptation of *Tess of the D'Urbervilles*, a story about a
rape victim , was not a Syndicate kind of gal. In fact, she
refused to sign with them, which meant that her company was closed out of performing in their theatres.
Because of the almost absolute power of the Syndicate,
the only other options for a non-Syndicate theatre company were church basements and masonic lodges. And
for years, until the Syndicate was trust-busted, that's
where one of the greatest actors in America performed.

And hence the quotation about her.

The price of being seated at the head of the table is very
high. It means that one must conform to the standards of
the host. But what does that chair at the end really signi-
fy? Isn't its status honorary, not geographic? That was the

secret that Minnie discovered. Her actions, like Eva Le Gallienne's, radically challenged the function of American theatre and a woman's place in it. She was aware of her own worth, considered artistic freedom the greatest privilege, and chose her venues accordingly. She redefined success, and in doing so, radically revised the guest list.

If we are true to ourselves, to our standards, and to our priorities, we can trust that the world—at least the part of it that is aligned with us—will find us wherever we are. Why should we care about anything else?

Priorities

"Hurry!"

—Donaldina Cameron

Donaldina Cameron was a woman in a hurry. She devoted her life to rescuing Chinese girls from enforced prostitution. To do this, she literally had to kidnap these girls, who were brought over as the legal "brides" of various pimps and gang members, and then kept in brothels in San Francisco. Some of these brides were as young as six. The girls were frequently introduced to opium and kept in drugged states for the "work" they were compelled to do. A girl with a venereal disease would be locked in a room with a knife. She could choose to starve to death or kill herself.

Donaldina's life was perpetually in danger, and her activity was technically illegal, since these girls were married to citizens. Undeterred by threats, she continued to follow up on anonymous tips and to go into Chinatown at all hours, climbing over roofs, down secret passages, and frequently carrying the drugged child in her arms.

Some of the girls had been warned about the "White Devil," as Donaldina was called, and they were terrified of her. Often they resisted their rescue, and occasionally they resisted rehabilitation in the Presbyterian mission where Donaldina housed and educated the girls.

On one occasion, Donaldina was scheduled to meet with the President to make her case for closing the loophole in immigration law that allowed the practice to exist. But while she was on her way to Washington, she stopped in

Chicago, and someone there smuggled her a message about a girl being held captive in that city. Donaldina dropped everything, forfeiting her chance to meet with the President, in order to rescue the girl.

Some might say it would have been wiser to sacrifice the one girl for the chance to change a law that might save hundreds. Obviously, this was not Donaldina's perspective. And if she had had a mind to weigh her options and jockey for an advantageous position, I doubt she would have been so successful in her many rescue missions.

What we can and can't negotiate is important. In a rush to avoid "black-and-white" thinking, it is easy to forget that often there is a grace in the moral absolute, a grace that enables us to rise above what seem to be impossible odds.

I could find no other quotations for Donaldina, because she was not a woman of words. The records of her life were the Chinese-American girls who became teachers, doctors, and reformers—and all because Donaldina had been in a hurry.

Passing

—————❊—————

" All of the complication of these last few years,—and
you can't guess what complications there have been,
darling child,—have been based on this business of
'passing.'"

—Jessie Redmon Fauset

This is a quotation from Angela Murray, the protagonist
of Jessie's 1928 novel, *Plum Bun*. Angela goes to New
York to taste life in the fast lane, which for her means
passing as white. As "Angele Mory," she dates the sons of
white millionaires, only to discover her lack of status in
their eyes as a woman. Her passing estranges her from
her own family and cuts her off from the excitement of
the Harlem Renaissance. In the end, she gives it up.

"Passing" is a term also applied to Lesbians and gay men
who are living in the world as if they are heterosexual.
Passing can be very tempting, especially when it is as
simple as taking advantage of people's assumptions.
Because Angela looked white, people assumed she had
an anglo-american background. Lesbians—unless we
have a strong butch appearance, and sometimes not even
then!—are assumed to be heterosexual unless we make
overt reference to our Lesbianism.

And there is passing in terms of class. Women can sit in
on discussions by class-privileged women, and if we do
not challenge expressions of classism, we will be
assumed to be one of them—or we will be seen as vali-
dating their value system, even if we are identified as
having a different background.

There is passing in terms of supporting the dominant culture. The radical feminist is rarely at home with the films or videos or television shows or popular novels of hetero-patriarchy. But when she is attending these or discussions of these by other Lesbians, does she risk being considered a party-pooper by sharing her perspective?

There is passing in terms of the way women tolerate unacceptable behavior from men and boys. I know that I spoke out about the injustice of placing middle school girls in a classroom with boys, because the boys' attention spans and interests were so radically different that it was impossible to meet the needs of both groups. Because the boys were so disruptive, I was compelled to teach to their interest level, creating an environment of compulsory underachievement for the girls. Although my supervisor acknowledged this was a common problem that everyone knew about, I was ostracized for naming it.

Many older women try to "pass" in terms of looking younger, because there are very real penalties, especially in hiring practices, against being older. Many women with hidden disabilities choose not to identify ourselves as disabled in certain environments.

When who we are is stigmatized in the culture (African American, Asian, Latina, Jewish, old, disabled, Lesbian, radical feminist, and so on), the temptation to pass—if we can—is always present. Every woman must find her own way with how she identifies herself and to whom. But if we could all "come out" collectively on all fronts, on the same day, I believe the world would never be the same.

Talking to Yourself

———»>«<———

"This is my letter to the World
That never wrote to Me..."

—Emily Dickinson

The path of the radical feminist can seem lonely. Some days it feels as if we are in the business of putting notes into bottles and tossing them into the ocean. Some days it may feel as if we're just talking to ourselves. And from that perception, it's a short skip and a hop to feeling as if we're crazy.

Talking to ourselves is a radical activity. Imagine the first woman who said that she was experiencing rape in her marriage. Imagine the first woman who said that the jokes in the office were harassment. Imagine the first girl who named her father as a rapist. Imagine the first girl who said that the boys' comments about her breasts were affecting the quality of her education.

That courage did not come out of mid-air. Those women and girls had been talking to themselves first. Even more radical, they were listening. And out of talking and listening to ourselves comes believing in ourselves. And out of believing in ourselves comes the courage to speak out our truth to a world in denial.

Emily Dickinson's poetry is profoundly anti-patriarchal. Only seven of her poems were published in her life-time—all without her name and some against her wish-es. Few people even knew the poems existed, and those who did, considered them quaint and eccentric. After she died, there they were: little handmade booklets tied together in the bottom drawer of her bureau. Like little bundles of dynamite.

Her early poems were edited to "fix" the grammar. Later, it was acknowledged that her radical use of the dash instead of more conventional punctuation was critical to the multiple readings of the lines and verses. Her so-called bad grammar was restored.

It took a long time for the world to discover Emily Dickinson and to appreciate her genius. She spent her life talking to herself. And because of what must have been excruciating years of isolation and self-doubt, her poems cut across more than a century to speak to women with the laser penetration of one woman's absolute unattenuated truth.

Seeing Clearly

"Do you mean I been treated good and can't sit down?"

—Fannie Lou Hamer

This is one of my favorite quotations.

In 1963, African American Civil Rights activist Fannie Lou Hamer was arrested at a bus station in Winona, Mississippi, on her way back from a voter registration training. She was severely beaten during her incarceration, but while she was still in jail, she was required to write out a statement that she had not been mistreated. The statement was dictated to her by a member of the Mississippi State Highway Patrol—a man with a gun. Fannie Lou was very clear about the danger of her situation, and she determined that her only course of resistance was to write the statement as poorly as she could—in order to be able to repudiate it later. It was during this dictation session, however, that she asked the question cited above.

I think of all the women in this culture who "can't sit down"—and not just the survivors of battering, but also the women who are on their feet all day as full-time workers at soul-destroying and physically debilitating jobs, the women who are single mothers, the Lesbians who are harassed and evicted—kept on the move constantly. I think of the women whose memories are so traumatic, they can't bear to pause and reflect on their lives. And I wish that we could all ask Fannie Lou's question with the same clarity about our symptoms and their cause.

Love

⸻⸻▶●◀⸻⸻

"I'm entering my forties with more simplistic criteria—
anyone with a greater capacity for love than I is a
valuable teacher. And when I look back on the body
of book reviews I've produced in the past fifteen
years, for all their socioideolitero brilliant somethin-
gorother, the underlying standard always seemed to
be — Does this author here genuinely love his/her
community?"

—Toni Cade Bambara

African American author Toni Cade Bambara loved her
community. She loved it in all its conflicts and contradictions. She loved it passionately during a time of wrench-
ing transition, when everything old was suddenly suspect, quickly discarded, easy to scorn. Her love for her
community pulses in every line of her writing. I am hard
put to imagine where she would find those teachers she
mentions — the ones with a greater capacity for loving
than herself!

In many ways, western so-called civilization is entering its
forties. As a planet, we are being compelled to turn toward
more simplistic criteria, as our resources diminish and the
sobering bill comes due for environmental arrogance.

It seems that we are experiencing a planetary mid-life crisis, with two movements occurring simultaneously: One
is a movement toward massive denial via electronic distraction, academic ultra-specialization, and media-
induced dissociation. The other is a movement toward
multi-cultural diversity, respect for life, amends to the
planet — simpler criteria.

It is a time when it is easy to become confused, over-whelmed, hornswoggled — and then passive, compliant, apathetic. There has never been such an array of sophisticated flim-flam men. Our own minds are being constantly programmed to turn against us.

Toni's quotation is like a magic sword we can take and use to cut our way through the tangle. "Does this person/activity/art/institution genuinely love his/her/its community?" Slice! One clean stroke. It doesn't take great intellectual analysis. It doesn't take massive knowledge of technical jargon. It takes a cultivation of our own love for our community, so that we can recognize the genuine article in others.

Judges

------◦◦◦------

"I, however, who belong to the founders of the
Independent Exhibition must stick to my principles,
our principles, which were, no jury, no medals, no
awards...

The truth is I have not served on the jury, never will
serve on a jury, nor be the means of repressing the
works of another painter. I think the whole system is
wrong... The jury system has proved a failure since
hardly a single painter of talent in the last fifty years in
France has not been a victim to the system — Among
those refused again and again, are Corot, Courbet,
Millet & hosts of others... We need a new system."

— Mary Cassatt

Mary Cassatt was discriminated against by reason of
gender, but also because her work broke with the conventions of the day. Later, when her work became recognized, she turned down the prestigious Lippincott Prize,
as she said, sticking to her principles.

Hers is a refreshing example of a woman who remembered her humiliations and frustrations after she
achieved success. Most of us know of the politics, nepo-
tism, and other power games behind supposedly merit-
based awards. We're very vocal about these insights
when we are rejected, but how often do we publicize this
knowledge when we are the recipients, and how often do
we turn down the award?

In the quotation, Mary calls for a new system. What
would it be?

Women in the visual arts have made little headway in the mainstream world of prestigious gallery shows. This is even more true for women of color.

Would the new system be one of quotas? Or special women's shows or women of color shows? Or would it be the discrediting and dismantling of the traditional powers-that-be who decide what has value and what does not? And what would that dismantling entail?

Those who determine the mainstream value of a work of art make up a sophisticated network of critics, journalists, art historians, gallery owners and museum curators, art investors, and brokers. This network is capable of change (witness the current popularity of Cassatt), but it changes very slowly—in most cases too slowly to help the individual artist.

Mary's "system" was not a bad one. She got together with the other artists rejected by the mainstream, and they held their own exhibition, the Independent Exhibition. These Independents came to be known later as the Impressionists, and collectively they constituted a movement. Insisting that they be judged by their own standards, they worked among themselves to develop their own theories and cultivate their own patrons.

Posturing as the misunderstood and unappreciated artist may be dramatic and personally cathartic, but a more effective strategy is organizing to become an insider of an outsiders' club.

Guns

────➤●◄────

"I feel that one had better die fighting against injustice than to die like a dog or a rat in a trap. I had already determined to sell my life as dearly as possible if attacked. I felt if I could take one lyncher with me, this would even up the score a little bit."

—Ida B. Wells-Barnett

Ida Wells was one of the first African Americans to speak out publicly against lynching. Lynching was a common terrorist tactic that white southerners employed against formerly enslaved African Americans in an effort to maintain white dominance in a social order that had been disrupted by the Emancipation Proclamation and Reconstruction. Periodic random lynchings had the same effect as rape does today. Members of the targeted caste get the message: Keep a low profile.

The mythology around lynching in the nineteenth century was also similar to the mythology around rape prior to the women's movement: The victims must have done something to provoke the attack. They must have been "asking for it." With lynching, the traditional mythology was that the victim had raped or otherwise "insulted the womanhood" of a white woman. With rape, of course, the mythology is that the woman teased or challenged the manhood of the rapist.

When Ida began her newspaper campaign to expose lynching for what it was, a hate crime, many of the rising middle-class Blacks separated themselves from her cause. They disassociated themselves from the victims, clinging to the myth that only "bad" Blacks got lynched.

In other words, it could never happen to them. Until recently, a similar phenomenon occurred whenever a woman or girl would speak out about her experience of rape or incest. Many women, although horrified by the violence, would react with questions designed to fix blame on the victim.

Oppressed people evolve strategies for surviving that do not always reflect solidarity within their sub-culture. In Ida's time, African Americans who told the truth about lynching were subject to threats, boycotts of their businesses, terrorism, and even lynching themselves. Ida's press was smashed and she was compelled to continue her work outside the South.

But she carried a gun and made a point of letting everyone know about it. Furthermore, she publicized her intention to use it, regardless of the odds against her. And Ida Wells lived a long life, dying of natural causes.

Why are so many women afraid to carry guns? Why is there a universally repeated myth that carrying a gun is more dangerous than not carrying one, that the assailant will take it and use it against us? Do women believe that naivete creates some kind of force field around us? That only other women get raped? Why is it that many women only take up arms after they have been assaulted?

Melanie Kaye/Kantrowitz, author of *The Issue Is Power*, suggests that if we are afraid of owning guns, we may be afraid of our own anger. She suggests that we may be taking the lives of our attackers more seriously than our own.

Strategy

"I cannot and will not cut my conscience to fit the
fashion of the time."

—Lillian Hellman

Lillian Hellman was a playwright called to testify before
the House Committee on Un-American Activities, under
the notorious communist witch-hunter Joseph McCarthy.
Her lover, Dashiell Hammett, had already gone before
them, refused to cooperate, and been sent to prison, where
he contracted serious health problems that eventually
resulted in his death.

Many women know that Lillian Hellman took a courageous stand, refusing to name the names of "known
Communists," the act that would purchase her own
immunity.

But what all went into that? Was she just superwoman?

Actually she was scared to death and very unsure of how
she would behave when the moment arrived. But she
took personal charge of the ordeal:

She left Dashiell at home, whose motivations for proph-
esying doom-and-gloom she did not altogether trust. She
did not tell him where in Washington she would be stay-
ing, because she didn't want to have to deal with any
demoralizing phone calls.

She met with her attorney, who at the very last minute
wanted her to completely reverse her strategy and settle
for a dangerous compromise. Even in the face of this massive betrayal of support, Lillian stood firm: It was simply

too late for her to change the plan.

Down to her last dollars and facing a prison sentence of unknown duration, she went out shopping and bought an expensive dress and some new gloves to wear to the hearing. She was performing rituals that felt "normal" and empowering to her. She refused to sit petrified in her hotel room, as if she were waiting to be called to the principal's office.

These are interesting choices Lillian made. She was not afraid to face the truth about her lover. She knew that Dashiell was not supportive of her achieving her goal of victory without compromise. He needed and wanted to see her share his fate, and he could not support the spiritual vision she was holding in thought. She knew she needed to get away from his negative influence.

She also was wise enough to refuse the "expert" counsel of her own attorney. She realized that even though he was supposed to be on her side, he was, in fact, carrying the germs of McCarthyism.

And she asserted her womanhood, which for her at that time, meant going out and buying an expensive dress and white gloves. She would go to the hearings on her own terms, dressing to please herself, to see and feel her power—the power of investing her last dollar in something that gave her pleasure.

The actual events at her hearing are fascinating. I recommend that the interested reader check out *Scoundrel Time*, her own account of that scurrilous chapter in patriarchal history.

Defacement

" ...drawing mustaches on other people's property..."

—Maya Lin

This is how Maya Lin described the "addition" to her design for the Vietnam Veterans Memorial in Washington, DC. Her design, two long black granite walls that meet to form a V, was specifically intended to avoid any "falsely heroic" statement about war in general, and this war in particular. The polished stone, carved with the names of the dead, acts as a mirror to reflect the images of the still-living back to themselves.

Her design was selected from a field of national entries, and the fact that the winner was a student (and only twenty-one!), an Asian American, and a female resulted in a storm of ageist, racist, and misogynist protest. The third-place runner-up (a male and former anti-war demonstrator) had designed a traditional statue of three soldiers brandishing a flag, and it was proposed that this be placed in the center of Maya's V. How's that for explicit? This was what she referred to as "drawing the mustache." Not only did it clash with the design elements, but the proposal would have completely subverted her intention for the memorial.

As a "compromise," the statue was placed 120 feet from her wall. Maya, the winner, received $20,000 for her design. The sculptor received more than $200,000 for his commission. His name was on the cover of the program at the dedication ceremony, and Maya's did not appear at all!

Historically, women scientists, inventors, and artists have seen our work "mustached" time and again. How can we survive the grief and rage of not only our personal violations, but also the violations of our art, of our ideas? Quite frankly, some women—the sculptor Camille Claudel, for instance—don't survive. Others, and happily Maya is one of them, not only survive, but go on to live lives of great productivity and achievement.

The Vietnam Veterans Memorial has become the most visited monument in Washington. Veterans have written copious testimonials (some to Maya personally) about the powerful healing they experience interacting with her design. In spite of her enemies' best efforts at sabotage, the work could not be separated from the spiritual qualities it embodied, and it has prevailed.

Although Maya Lin's life was temporarily derailed by all the controversy and fame, she went on to design the Civil Rights Memorial in Montgomery and the Women's Table, a monument commemorating the centennial of Yale's admission of women into their graduate school.

The Lesbian poet Sappho had insight into the durability of her art: "You may forget but/ Let me tell you/ this: someone in/ some future time/ will think of us." Indeed. Although her work was deliberately destroyed, fragments surfaced two thousand years later as mummy wrappings uncovered by archeologists in the 1920's.

Traps

―――――◆◆◆――――

"Manasa lamba manify: atao mafy, rovitra; atao male-my, tsy afa-tseroka."

[Like washing thin fabric: wash it hard and it will tear; wash it gently and you will not get the dirt out.]

—Malagasy proverb

This is the perennial challenge for the radical.

People are always asking us to keep our voices down, to frame our arguments within the currently fashionable social context, to respect the "diversity" of others, even when that "diversity" is bought with our oppression.

People tell us they can't hear what we're saying when we shout, but when we speak in measured tones, we find that they never listen.

People tell us to keep our arguments within the perimeters of the panel topic, the conference theme, the guidelines for the anthology, and so forth, when these perimeters are specifically designed to keep us marginalized and on the defensive. For example, how much valuable Lesbian energy has been wasted trying to prove that we're just like everyone else, when the real issue is the immorality of compulsory heterosexualism? And how about the boundary against "reverse discrimination," which is, in fact, the retaining wall of colonialism?

People tell us we must respect the diversity of opinions if we want our own position to be respected. How can we do this when this so-called "diversity" includes all kinds of complicity with a system that is destroying us?

And so we wash the fabric gently and we "soil ourselves with timid conservatism" (Mary Baker Eddy), or we rub folks the wrong way hard enough to bring their underlying prejudices to the surface—and in doing so, we tear the social fabric of our interactions.

And so the choice is between dirty secrets and ruptured relationships. Each woman must choose in her own time and judging by her own strength. And maybe, over time, we can evolve a social fabric strong enough to stand the process—either that, or women with the moral fiber to resist the taint of patriarchy.

Empathy

Women are fixers. We feel a need to prove our value, since patriarchy has taught us that women have no intrinsic worth. Whenever we hear of a woman who has lost her home, many of us have impulses to offer her our spare room, our living-room couch—or even to take the couch ourselves and offer her our bed!

But often these "helpful gestures" are anything but. Sometimes they are tests, to see if the other person will take advantage of our poor boundaries, so that we can then position them in our lives as yet another abuser. And, yes, there can be some power in that set-up. They will be in our debt, and we may even be exempted from account-ability toward them, since they are now the designated abuser.

Or, sometimes, the "helpful gesture" is designed to mask the fact that we really don't care, that we are in a syn-thetic and socially-dictated relationship to them, and this is our way to buy out of genuine interaction.

Maybe the "helpful gesture" is a way to soothe our own anxieties about a world where homelessness, poverty, unemployment, and abandonment by lovers abound. It may be we ourselves who are finding the situation unbearable, and not the woman who is actually experi-encing it. Maybe we are using the "helpful gesture" as a charm to prevent the same fate from happening to us.

I think of a poem by Marianne Moore, where she says that restraint is the greatest indicator of deep emotions.

The more we are really feeling for the other, the more we need to restrain our first impulses, so that we can really hear the woman and also allow her to define her needs to us, which may be very different from what we are anticipating. Often, she just needs to be heard.

Incest

"Tonight, I stand before you, an incest survivor. A list of all my accomplishments together—times 100, pales before the only real accomplishment of my life—said in only three words. I survived incest."

—Marilyn Van Derbur

Marilyn Van Derbur was the 1958 Miss America. She was Phi Beta Kappa, a workaholic, and a successful motivational speaker. She has helped found the Kempe Adult Survivors Program to educate families about incest, and especially about the terrible price survivors pay when they are denied therapy or forced to repress the memory of their experience.

Incest survivors experience syndromes similar to the post-traumatic stress disorder that was first identified among war veterans and survivors of terrorist incidents, such as kidnapping. But for children, who were hostages and prisoners of war during the time when we were just beginning to formulate our ideas about who we were and what the world was like, our PTSD can be a chronic syndrome that has affected every aspect of our lives. The adult survivor of trauma must relearn trust. The child survivor must build it from scratch.

Surviving incest, recovering memories, confronting perpetrators and enablers, and learning healthy boundaries, functional coping skills, and trust are remarkable achievements, especially in a society that is not particularly invested in the telling of family secrets. The world is more likely to point to income, titles, property ownership, or awards as measures of success. It's important for those of us who have survived incest to appreciate our healing work as *real work,* and to know that, like Marilyn Van Derbur, this work may well be our most important. It may also be the most critical work for the rest of the planet. When we can collectively confront incest as the central paradigm for patriarchy, it will lose the secrecy that constitutes its foundation—and the whole system will fall like a house of cards.

Teaching

—————>◦◦◦◦<—————

"What office is there which involves more responsibility, which requires more qualifications, and which ought, therefore, to be more honourable, than that of teaching?"

—Harriet Martineau

Indeed. Harriet Martineau, nineteenth-century feminist and social critic, hit the nail on the head.

And the younger and more impressionable the children, the more crucial the quality of education. Teachers of small children have the greatest responsibilities of all. And yet, in patriarchy, day care and pre-school teachers are granted less status than the teachers of older children or adults. By less status, I mean less pay, because let's face it—the bottom line of value in terms of this society is money.

There is a hierarchy in education, where the "higher" up you go—that is, the older the students and the more formal the institutions, the more specialized the training and the better the renumeration. Seemingly the specialization is the rationale for the higher pay: The more unique the services you can offer, the more money you can command in a market economy.

But the education of very young children requires more specialization than the acquiring of most PhD's. In order to teach children, it's important to understand their stages of development, their perspectives of the world, their intellectual and moral capacities, and their interests and needs. And children grow and change rapidly when they are young. The teacher must constantly customize her curriculum to these changing needs—and to the individual child! In addition to being an expert on child psychology and pedagogy, she needs to have excellent mental hygiene herself.

The presence of young children is a trigger for unrecovered survivors. If we were ignored, neglected, criticized harshly, or pushed to achieve when we were children, and if we have not been through a process of acknowledging the abusiveness of those practices, the harm they did us, and the repressed feelings they generated—well, it's almost a sure bet we're going to practice those same abuses on the children in our lives—especially if we have authority over them. The recent attention to sexual abuse in day care situations is tragic evidence of adults acting out on children in their care.

And, because the care of small children demands so much unconditional giving on the part of the adult caregiver, teachers of these children have the greatest need for summers off, paid vacation time, and sabbaticals. It's too easy to become burnt out or, worse, numbed out by the care of children.

What would happen if pre-school teaching was considered the most prestigious, the most elite field in education? What if only the very best, healthiest women could attain these jobs? And what if the pay was commensurate with this status?

Love

———»•«———

" ... women who want without needing are expensive
and sometimes wasteful, but women who need without wanting are dangerous—they suck you in and
pretend not to notice."

—Audre Lorde

These are the words of African American Lesbian poet
Audre Lorde. They are taken from her remarkable autobiography *Zami: A New Spelling of My Name*.

Two women who want one another can negotiate. Two
women who need one another can certainly cement a
bond. A woman who wants and a woman who needs can
strike a terrorist's bargain.

But where is the place for love in all this wanting and
needing? And if wanting and needing are not conducive
to genuine loving, then who in this life is ever going to be
free enough from want or need to be able to love?

Or is it possible to experience want and need, but to exercise a moral discipline strong enough to keep these from
contaminating a relationship based on genuine affection,
respect, and shared interests?

What does it take to see an area where another woman
can be manipulated and to refrain from exploiting that
weakness? What does it take to encourage another
woman to challenge her fears and to go after her
dreams—even when her quest might mean leaving you
behind?

What it takes is a strong sense of morality, a deep desire

to do to one's partner as one would have done to oneself, and a profound commitment to honesty and fairness—either that or a long history of obsessive-compulsive, controlling, manipulative, and possessive relationships that have all blown up in one's face.

It seems to me that a lover should be like a catalyst in one's life, creating conditions for reactions and transformation in the partner, but not participating in these reactions herself. For a lover to continue to catalyze growth, she must maintain her integrity and autonomy. Her partner may be brought up short by her own fears, or her own limitations, or her own expectations, or by all kinds of ghosts from her past—but these are about changes and interactions within herself. And she may seek out therapists or friends or support groups for processing her changes, but, it seems to me, that the more the lover's role is considered as catalyst, the better the chances for a strong and flexible friendship in which the partners will not exploit one another.

Rights

"Allegedly, inclusion in the U.S. gave us 'rights,' the much-prized individual rewards that Americans wave in the faces of their conquered peoples, like little American flags on the graves of fallen soldiers. Universal suffrage, private property, and public education are among these 'rights,' as are the trumpeted joys of mass consumption, mass communication, and mass popular culture... By 'rights,' Americans do not mean natives controlling their own affairs, holding their land and resources collectively as a people rather than as individuals, or learning and transmitting their own Native language, religion, and family structure."

—Haunani-Kay Trask

Haunani-Kay Trask is an activist for Hawaiian sovereignty. She points out how the reality of imperialism gives the lie to the ideology about "rights."

Patriarchy systematically strips our humanity in the name of an artificial system, and then it doles out counterfeits and caricatures of this stolen humanity—our so-called rights. And in exercising these "rights," we become complicitous in the rape of the environment, in the pitting of races, genders, age groups, and so forth against one another and in our own brainwashing.

In her writing, Haunani-Kay emphasizes the importance of *mana* in the Native Hawaiian movement for self-determination:

"...the defining characteristic of leadership is *mana*, the ability to speak for the people and the land, to command respect by virtue of this ability, and to set the issues of public debate as those which benefit the *lahui* [the nation]..."

"In this decolonizing context, *mana* as an attribute of leadership is at once a tremendous challenge to the colonial system which defines political leadership in terms of democratic liberalism, that is, in terms of electoral victory, as well as a tremendous challenge to aspiring Hawaiian leaders who want to achieve sovereignty."

"... on the front lines, in the glare of public disapproval, are our women—articulate, fierce, and culturally grounded. A great coming together of women's *mana* has given birth to a new form of power based on a traditional Hawaiian belief: women asserting their leadership for the sake of the nation."

And these women are operating outside the patriarchal systems of political power. They operate outside of them, not only because these systems are hostile to women, but also because the values represented by patriarchy are deeply antagonistic to the exercise of *mana*. The women would have to forfeit their Native leadership in order to practice any form of leadership sanctioned by a colonial system.

This naming and understanding of an alternative source of power, one intrinsic to one's native identity, is a very, very powerful tool for liberation. And that power goes hand-in-glove with disenfranchisement from the dominant system.

76

Heroism

"Heroism is the *only* alternative."

—Phyllis Chesler

Phyllis Chesler, pioneer in the field of women's mental health and author of the ground-breaking *Women and Madness*, made this statement in reference to the oppression of women.

Heroism implies marked courage or daring, self-sacrifice and acts that are supremely noble, but when the alternatives are denial, appeasement, betrayal, compromise, and self-abasement—does that definition hold true?

Leaping from a tenth story window into a net might appear heroic or radical, but when the building is on fire, when the room is filling with toxic smoke, and when death is immanent—the leap requires more of a reasonable assessment of the situation than any tremendous courage or daring. It requires an understanding of the alternatives—or lack thereof—that renders risk preferable to sure annihilation.

Where this analogy breaks down in its application to women is the issue of "sure annihilation." So many of our mothers, our grandmothers, our sisters, our daughters have been sexually, spiritually, artistically, intellectually, and physically annihilated that we may have difficulty envisioning the possibility of escape. We may even have difficulty seeing this destruction as annihilation. It may look like the natural course of events, or an inevitable concomitant to the process of growing up. It may even look self-inflicted.

Women like Phyllis Chesler, whose books provide an analysis of the war against women, help us to understand that it *is* annihilation, and that there *is* an alternative. Perhaps if we could help foster in one another a proper horror of death by asphyxiation, we might be less intimidated by that daring leap from patriarchy's burning building.

Food

"You are what you eat."

We have all heard the expression. But have we really considered the radical implications of living in defiance of this adage?

I have serious issues with $100-a-fifty-minute-hour therapists who are willing to bilk their clients week after week for years on end, pretending to address their mental health issues, when they have never made the slightest inquiry about their client's nutrition, recreational habits, or alcohol or drug use.

A friend of mine sees a very expensive therapist every week, and she also takes an expensive daily anti-depressant. The woman smokes cigarettes and indulges in a high-carbohydrate diet with low protein intake, small amounts of fresh fruit, and no fresh vegetables. She does not have a regular exercise program. No wonder she has trouble getting out of bed! How dare her therapist delude this woman into believing that she can experience vitality and positive momentum in her life by ignoring and abusing her body! How dare she!

I have another friend who is a counselor, and she has also been seeing a therapist for several years. This woman has a dependency on alcohol, and drinks almost every day. The issue has never, in three years of weekly therapy, been brought up. How serious is this therapist about her client's problems?

No, a good diet will not automatically enable an incest

survivor to access and integrate her memories. A good diet will not solve problems in relationships. Quitting smoking will not automatically change patterns developed through years of negative thinking. But when the body is so chronically undersupplied with nutrients that it must feed off its own tissue, how can a woman feel empowered to face the challenges of living in patriarchy? When she gets through her day with caffeine and sugar rushes, followed by low blood-sugar crises, her chances for stability and emotional serenity are almost nil, no matter who she turns it over to. When she has made her body a toxic waste dump for nicotine and alcohol, her immune system is already on overload, and if she doesn't get regular exercise, even more toxins will accumulate in the tissues. And of course, habitual recourse to numbing agents will deprive anyone of motivation to face the painful stimuli that indicate the need to change our lives.

I know women who would never skip an oil change for their car, but who have been running for years without essential fatty acids in their bodies. I know women who will ask the neighbor to start their car periodically if they must be away for a long trip, and yet they will go for months without any aerobic exercise themselves.

How radical is it to treat our cars better than our bodies?

Mental Vitamins

<hr/>

"My parents gave us a fantastic sense of security nd worth. By the time the bigots got around to telling us we were nobody, we already *knew* we were somebody."

—Florynce Kennedy

I remember reading an account by South Vietnamese prisoners-of-war, in which they told about passing coded messages back and forth by tapping on pipes that ran through their cell. The narrator referred to these messages as "mental vitamins."

Mental vitamins... It sounds as if African American Civil Rights attorney and activist Florynce Kennedy was raised with some great emotional nutrition!

What about those of us with deficiencies and toxicities from the emotional diets of our childhood—diets of criticism, ridicule, physical, and sexual abuse? Can we heal? I believe we can, but not without heavy emotional supplements in the areas of these deficiencies.

Gloria Steinem has described her idea of a women's "power lunch," where the participants (office workers, in her example) tell one another how wonderful they are and how much they appreciate the qualities they see in one another. That would certainly be a nourishing counter-balance to a work environment where working class women are taken for granted and exploited.

And what about support groups specifically focused on praise, recognition, encouragement?

Can we learn to call our friends and let them know that we need to be reminded of our worth, of the importance of our work, of our progress so far? It's too easy in patriarchy to become fooled into thinking everything we have done has been a waste of time. Can we learn to spot our deficiencies and go after those "mental vitamins?"

Can we tell our friends who may be too critical, that we need for them to express appreciation of who we are *right now*? Can we learn to avoid the "junk food" contacts, the "caffeine rush" interactions that leave us more depleted than before we indulged?

And can we learn to think about ourselves and talk to ourselves in ways that will give us energy and a sense of well-being?

Truth

"We have strength in proportion to our apprehension
   of the truth, and our strength is not lessened by
   giving utterance to truth."

—Mary Baker Eddy

The ways of the spirit are not the ways of the flesh.

Frequently, the world would tell us that apprehension of
the truth is overwhelming—that a life of denial is the best
way to keep our strength up. Certainly it seems that
many inveterate truth-tellers have collapsed from
exhaustion.

Mary Baker Eddy, the nineteenth-century founder of
Christian Science, a religion that challenged the patriarchal notions about a male god and a divinely human son,
speaks of the truth as a spiritual reality—one that is
beyond the horrific truths of rape, child abuse, battering,
disease, famine, war. In her theology, a spiritual perfection underlies the changing forms we experience as material existence. Her leading tenet is that the senses cannot
report accurately on the nature of reality, and that the
understanding of this will enable us to experience lives
closer to the spiritual ideal.

An arresting proposition. But is it just another form of
positive thinking, of self-delusion and denial? For Mary
Baker Eddy, the incontrovertible proof of her theory lay
in the ability to heal in defiance of the laws of matter.

It has been challenging for me to believe that telling the
truth is empowering. On the face of it, truth-telling has
cost me housing, jobs, and friends. But I do believe this

statement is true, and what has moved is my definition of empowerment. It no longer resides in concepts about material structures or human employment or affinities between personalities. And I find that I do, as the quotation says, grow in strength as I learn to let these things go and surrender control over the logistics of my human experience.

There is no way to test a theorem like this, except to live it—but I have found it a valuable support for radical activism.

Inheritance

—————

"The tyrant grinds down on his slaves and they don't turn against him; they crush those beneath them."

—Emily Brontë

These words echo one of the themes of Emily's famous novel, *Wuthering Heights*. In the book, Heathcliffe, once an abused child, grows up to become a terrible tyrant wreaking revenge on second generation members of the family who shamed him growing up.

There are marked similarities in the stories of Heathcliffe and Emily's father, Patrick. Both were from poverty class backgrounds, and both came under the patronage of wealthy men. In Patrick's case, his patron was responsible for Patrick being accepted at a prestigious university, where, a good scholar, he was nevertheless treated as a social outcast by the other boys, most of whom came from upper class families. Never really able to move away from his class origins, Patrick became a minister in the rural and remote parish of Haworth. He was rejected by his sweetheart.

Heathcliffe was "adopted" into an upper class family, where he had the misfortune to fall in love with Catherine Linton, a sister figure to him as a child. Her rejection of him set him on his lifelong course of revenge that makes up the body of the book.

Was Emily writing about her own family? Was she telling a story of family shame passed on to the next generation? Two of her sisters died from abusive conditions at a school for clergymen's daughters. Emily bonded closely with Branwell, her only brother, and she nursed him over the years as he struggled with his terrible dependency on alcohol, a dependency that killed him in his early thirties. Emily contracted an illness at his funeral and, refusing medication, she died just three months later.

What about the chain of oppression? As they say in AA, "pass it back or pass it on." How does one pass it back? Well, confronting the tyrant. Or, if the tyrant is dead, one can tell the story, as perhaps Emily did. But failing to confront or tell, one risks repressing or denying the history of pain. And when that happens, the subconscious—ever seeking closure—will cause one to act out the story, and pass on the pain.

Asking for Help

"My mind is overtaxed. Brave and courageous as I
am I feel that creeping on of that inevitable thing, a
breakdown, if I cannot get some immediate relief. I
need somebody to come and get me."

—Mary McLeod Bethune

These are the words of Mary McLeod Bethune, a seemingly indefatigable African American organizer, educator,
writer, and activist.

How many radical women have the wisdom to know
when we need help? How many of us have taken care to
surround ourselves with allies we can turn to when we
need this kind of help? And how many of us have the
courage to spell out exactly what it is we need?

The radical activist is already engaged in achieving the
unprecedented and often the seemingly impossible. To stop
and ask, "Can I do it?" or "Is this too much?" may feel like
opening one's flank to the enemy. Many of us adopt a
superwoman "can-do" attitude and then leave it up to our
bodies to set the boundaries. And our bodies will set these
boundaries by emotionally sabotaging key working
alliances or by staging physical breakdowns.

A second problem is the fact that many of us surround ourselves with those who will not challenge our actions. Let's
face it, we've got enough challenges! But this is self-defeat-
ing in the end, because the more beleaguered the activist,
the more she needs input from strong and independently-
minded women who will not be afraid to point out the
lapses in our perspective or the imbalances in our situation.

Jealousy

———✦———

"It was a newer crisis in Rosamond's experience... she was under the first great shock that had shattered her dream-world in which she had been easily confident of herself and critical of others; and this strange unexpected manifestation of feeling in a woman whom she had approached with shrinking aversion and dread, as one who must necessarily have a jealous hatred towards her, made her soul totter all the more with the sense that she had been walking in an unknown world which had just broken in upon her."

—George Eliot

Thus writes George Eliot of the climactic moment of *Middlemarch*.

What has just happened is that Rosamond, braced for a jealous and vindictive encounter with Dorothea—whom she sees as a rival, has instead been touched by Dorothea's warm and sincere concern for her welfare. In fact, Dorothea is sitting next to her, has taken off her gloves, and has reached out to hold Rosamond's hand.

This is, of course, science fiction. The patriarchal woman does not melt under the warm rays of Lesbian sisterhood. In fact, she is most likely to recover from her shock with a feeling of contempt for her rival's apparent failure to press her advantage.

In George Eliot's novel—and she has taken 726 pages to build to this point—Rosamond is forever changed by the encounter, responding with near adoration of the saintly Mrs. Casaubon and confessing her own unworthy motivations.

Dorothea Casaubon, the protagonist, is obviously George Eliot's alter-ego. She is a generous and high-minded woman, plain in appearance, more interested in social reform than fashion, and an intellectual companion to men instead of their sex object. As Dorothea is self-possessed and inhabits a realm of ideas, it does not occur to her to be jealous of other women. What do they have that she could possibly want?

I cite this passage, because it always touches me. A chapter later there is the obligatory reunion with the appropriate prince charming, the inevitable marriage, and so forth, but this is clearly the high point of the book, written in such trembling and fervent prose that one can sense the author's profound yearning for a real-life enactment. The scene is designed specifically to serve as an antidote for the cruelty and suffering that heterosexual women have inflicted on women not identified with their culture, and although it is a great and "feminine" mistake to believe that moral integrity will effect a change of heart in our tormentors, still there is a sweetness to this vision of sisterhood, coming as it does from the depth of George Eliot's great and woman-loving heart.

A breach of justice in our lives, like a washed-out bridge, can halt our momentum. Reconstructing that bridge through any means—even fantasy—can enable us to move forward again, because there is some part of our minds that is as satisfied by the fable as by reality. This is our salvation as well as our curse. How many women are living their lives through regency romances and *Days of Our Lives?* How many Lesbians through Naiad novels?

In using fantasy to heal our broken hearts, we must not abandon the radical vision that alone has the power to sustain us.

Usefulness

"Use is the highest law of our being, and it cannot be disobeyed with impunity."

—Lydia Maria Child

There is a difference between being useful and serving others. Feeling that one is being useful is a subjective state. Serving others is an objective state. The one places the ability to name outside the self, while the other locates it within the value system of the individual.

Lydia Maria Child struggled with this dichotomy all her life. Married to David Lee Child, she attempted to reconcile her role as faithful helpmate to her deadbeat husband with her radical calling as an anti-racist, feminist activist.

Maria wrote the first anti-slavery document in America, *An Appeal in Favor of that Class of Americans Called Africans*. Its publication in 1833 resulted in financial ruin of her successful children's magazine (the first in America) and social ostracization. Two years later, she published *The History of the Condition of Women in Various Ages and Nations*.

Ever the pragmatist, however, she also wrote a best-selling book on home economics, *The Frugal Housewife*, and *The Mother's Book*, which contained radical advice about educating girls about their sexuality. In 1865, she wrote *The Freedman's Books*, citing examples of African American heroism.

Maria's vision and intellectual gifts were prodigious, but it was her brother who was the professor at Harvard, and, although she was the breadwinner for her family, it was her husband who traveled overseas for the cause of abolition while Maria kept the home fires burning.

But if Maria was not strong enough to resist her conditioning, at least she did not pass it on. She became an important role model for the young Lesbian sculptor Harriet Hosmer, at a very critical juncture in Harriet's career. Hatty Hosmer was the only remaining child of her widower father, and although he had encouraged her interest in a non-traditional field, he was determined that Hatty should stay at home and content herself with a studio added on to the back of the house—a ladies' room, as it were, for a dilettante sculptress.

But Hatty listened to Maria, who could advise her from personal experience about the dangers of such a course. She and Hatty spent time visiting museums and theatres in Boston, and Maria's radical ideas must have had significant impact on the young artist, because Hatty left Boston with the internationally-renowned Lesbian actor Charlotte Cushman and took up residence with her in Rome, where, against her father's wishes, she established herself as a professional sculptor, operating a large studio and supervising a dozen male assistants.

Patriarchy obscures proper use, especially for women who are trained to be domestic and sexual slaves. In fact, many women feel it is subversive to even question that there might be some other use or purpose to their lives. How many women feel guilty about taking a dance class, or stealing away from their families to do a little writing or painting? And what about the woman who was a top athlete in her youth? Does she feel that has relevance to her role as an adult?

Finding our use may be taboo. Either that, or our use may

be so specialized that the field or market for it does not yet exist. This latter situation makes for a more difficult diagnosis. How can you know how you want to use yourself, if your real heart's desire is something that's never been done? So, yes, the right to be useful on one's own terms will require a fight. On the other hand, allowing others to use you is just about the worst thing in the world.

Violence vs. Non-Violence

"I hit them with the truth, and it hurts them."
—Fannie Lou Hamer

Fannie Lou Hamer was one of the earliest and fiercest Civil Rights workers in the United States. A sharecropper from Sunflower County, Mississippi, she began working with the Student Non-Violent Coordinating Committee (SNCC) in 1962 on voter registration drives, and from that time, up until her death from cancer in 1977, she was at the forefront of the struggle for African American rights—demonstrating, organizing, getting arrested, lobbying, suing, fund-raising, giving speeches, and singing at rallies, conferences, and conventions.

How effective a weapon is truth against an enemy who is armed and violent, dishonest, and irrational? What is the price of "turning the other cheek?" Malcolm X believed it was necessary to meet violence with violence, to speak to the white man in his own language—the language of the gun. And the militant Black Panther movement scared the wits out of white people precisely because it was in the language of dominance that they understood. Whites who had seen no reason to negotiate with Martin Luther King, suddenly found themselves faced with what they perceived as a much worse alternative.

Fannie Lou Hamer, a deeply spiritual woman, was committed to non-violence, but she was supportive of Malcolm X and appeared at rallies with him. Although she believed in loving her enemies, she never protected them. She never hesitated to speak out against injustice, whether it was on the local level or the national one. She spoke with an uncompromising voice about sexism and classism within the Civil Rights Movement itself. Her commitment to non-violence was a commitment to courage at a time before African Americans had any institutionalized power. And her commitment to non-violence did not save her from a brutal beating, from constant threats, and from several attempts on her life.

The question of whether to practice armed resistance or passive resistance is a difficult one. One hears how meeting violence with violence will make one "as bad as they are," or how the media will deliberately confuse resistance with aggression if violence is resorted to. And certainly, one has only to look at what happens to women who kill their batterers to know that there is truth behind this observation.

On the other hand, how many women died from practicing principles of passive resistance with their batterers? Is passive resistance an enlightened spiritual practice or a form of self-deception, an elaborate rationale for acting out victim behaviors? Just how effective is it to "speak truth to power" when one does not have the material clout to back up that truth—or even to protect oneself from the repercussions of telling that truth?

Every woman must find her own place in the liberation struggle. Perhaps the issue is not one of violent resistance versus passive resistance, but an issue of *integrity* of resistance—of finding the form that has the most integrity for the individual who practices it. Perhaps it is the *wholeness* of our truth that hurts the enemy.

Courage

"Courage is the price that Life exacts for granting peace."
—Amelia Earhart

In patriarchy, you can't expect to have your cake and eat it. The woman who chooses the path of least resistance is probably trading self-realization for security—and by security, I mean the absence of active resistance to her so-called choices. What security is there in not living up to one's potential, in not fulfilling one's dreams? Whatever this woman is trying to prevent—can it be worse than that?

The child inside us is hardier than the adult. She survives silencing, brainwashing, terrorism. She lives on for years, even when our adult selves have become collaborators in shutting her out. She bides her time.

The child inside us resists the pruning of patriarchy. Just as a tree, no matter how carefully trained and trimmed, will grow in response to its own wild and secret ways as soon as it is left alone—so will the child have her way just as soon as the adult weakens her control.

And beware the mid-life crisis, the point in time when the denial systems of our youth begin to break down and the agenda of the neglected child exerts itself like a long-repressed people turning on their colonizers!

If the truth were known about our processes, it would be understood that it takes less courage to live courageous-ly than to choose a path of cowardice and compromise, because there is no guarantee that the system to which we may have given our lives will hold up its promises (the plant may close, the husband may leave, social security may run out, the banks may fail)—and also because the child inside us, whose life we may be sidetracking, *always* finds a way to make us pay and pay and pay.

Supreme Court Resolutions

—————

"Resolved, That all laws as conflict, in any way, with the true and substantial happiness of woman, are contrary to the great precept of nature and of validity, for this is "superior in obligation to any other."

—Seneca Falls Resolutions

This was the first resolution of the nine Seneca Falls Resolutions drafted by Susan B. Anthony and presented at the Women's Rights Convention in 1848 in Seneca Falls, New York.

What a world it would be if there were a Supreme Court of Women, and women had the right to challenge any law under hetero-patriarchy on the grounds of this resolution!

And what a world it would be if every woman had her own interior "supreme court" to which she could appeal the unjust edicts even of her own making! How many of our obligations, our chores, our routines, our relationships would need to be overturned in favor of this superior law of nature, the law of women's happiness?

Integrity

———⟫●⟪———

"I cannot live without my life."

—Emily Brontë

What a self-evident statement! And yet millions of women—the majority, in fact—are attempting to do just that!

We are living the lives patriarchy has told us we want. We are living the lives we saw our mothers live. We are living the lives we saw on television growing up. We are living the lives we believe our children need us to live. We are living the lives our neighbors approve. We are living the lives that we have grown to believe are the safest thing for us.

And what is a woman who is not living her life? Seemingly happier and, at least superficially, better adjusted in patriarchy than a woman who is being true to herself. The woman not living her life is screening out the memories and perceptions that are not appropriate to the character she is playing. And wouldn't that be a relief? She doesn't have to know that her father used her, that her husband is unfaithful, that her children are abusive toward her. She doesn't have to register the ongoing assaults on her integrity from the mass media. She doesn't have to know her job is meaningless, that the entire system of government is designed to disenfranchise her, that the acts of violence that flood the newspapers could all be meant for her. She doesn't have to know these things, because they belong to real life, and she is only concerned with her script.

She is present for her boss, present for her family, present for her community, present for her church. She may even be present for a number of wonderful environmental or even "feminist" causes. In fact, she is probably more present in the external world than the radical feminist who requires every ounce of her own energy just to be present to herself.

Would that we all had Emily's integrity! What a different world it would be if women truly could not live without our lives.

Enduring

"Children's talent to endure stems from the ignorance
of alternatives."

—Maya Angelou

Unfortunately, many children grow up without revising
this "talent to endure" in light of adult options.

As a Lesbian-feminist playwright, what I see is a colossal
ignorance of alternatives in the art and lives of women. I
am thinking of the number of films and plays where the
woman's only alternative to an abusive situation is madness or suicide.

A 1980's film, *Thelma and Louise*, was considered a water-
shed by many, because the heroines actually fought
back—and fought back creatively and with a certain
amount of relish. But what happens to the women who
act up? The screenwriter literally drew a blank, and her
heroines, with the police in hot pursuit, took the "option"
of driving over the edge of the Grand Canyon. After that,
the screen went white. I can't tell you how many women
assured me that this was a positive, even triumphant
ending!

So how do we train ourselves, as formerly abused children, as molested girls, as battered women, to learn the
alternatives, or to believe they must exist even when we
can't see them?

We can support the women's art that imagines these
alternatives for us. We can learn to brainstorm and day-
dream with one another. We can develop a spiritual discipline to help break through the mesmeric miasma of

despair generated around the clock by patriarchy.

And we can learn to step back and ask questions about our "talent to endure," of which, by the way, we may be quite proud. Is making tons of money at a woman-hating job really success? Is being the dominant partner in a relationship really empowering? Is it a spiritual practice to "do without," or are we too afraid to make demands on life?

Maya Angelou, an African American writer, was an abused child who endured. But, more significant, she became an adult woman who thrived.

Love

Pay attention to anything the patriarchy does a lot of.

One of the things with which we are inundated is propaganda about romance: love-at-first-sight, "my world is empty without you," "the overpowering feeling/ That any second you may suddenly appear..."

If the patriarchy approves it, then it must be a trap. Interesting how many radical Lesbians exempt romantic love from their critique of patriarchal institutions and embrace the myth wholeheartedly—despite the fact it makes us miserable, diverts our precious dyke energy, and turns us into the worst kind of emotional consumers and sexual addicts.

Anais Nin was primed for romance. She was raised in an incestuous environment and went on to "choose" a series of father figures as her lovers: Henry Miller, her therapist, and—horrifyingly, her own father when she was an adult.

How can you be loved for who you are, until you are being who you are? Too many women have been brainwashed to put the cart before the horse. We have been taught to go after love, to court it, to lure it, to ensnare it. And once we have what we think is love (usually just compatible co-dependency), we are taught to adjust our personas to become someone who will be able to maintain that so-called love for ever—even if it's the wrong person in the wrong place at the wrong time for the wrong reasons! (That's just how unlovable we must be.)

We have not been taught to discover ourselves through a series of bold risks and crushing failures. We have not been taught to make mistakes, uproot, start over, make messes, get it right. We have not learned to focus on ourselves, on our agenda, and trust that the appropriate companions will appear on the road with us as we move toward our goals. And we have not learned to stay on that road even when our boon companions must take the turn-off.

For many years, Anais was seeking validation from what her captors had trained her to believe would be her only source of self-worth: older so-called mentors who would use her sexually. Instead, her validation came from her writing, from seeing herself think. And out of this commitment to herself, she found her way out of victimization.

Reverse Discrimination

—————◆————

"There is no analogy whatever among men, however
certain classes of men may be, to the wholesale
destruction which goes on from year to year among
women."

—attributed to Josephine Butler

"Men suffer from patriarchy, too." How often do we have
to listen to this whenever any issue about women's
oppression is brought up?

Josephine Butler was an activist against the Contagious
Diseases Acts in England. Under this law, women who
were out walking after dark without male escorts could
be taken into custody and forced to undergo a "medical
examination" for venereal disease. Josephine accurately
described the practice as "rape with a steel phallus."

At the time when she was agitating for reform, the patriarchy viewed prostituted women as lustful, evil and
predatory—victimizing men, by undermining their
morals and infecting them with diseases. This, unfortunately, is not an outdated notion. Recently, Lee Wuornos,
a prostituted woman, was sentenced to Death Row for
shooting a man who handcuffed her, anally raped her
against her will, poured alcohol into the wounds he
inflicted, and told her that he was going to murder her
and then rape her again, implying that he had done this
before and found it just as satisfying. At the trial, Lee was
characterized as a man-hater, a vicious pervert who deliberately used sex to ensnare her victims and then kill them.
Testimony about the criminal record of her "victim" was
not allowed into the record. Outrageous.

Our "brothers" in the abolitionist fight, our "brothers" in the labor movement, our "brothers" in the anti-war movement, our "brothers" in the AIDS awareness campaign—where have they been for women's rights? Few male abolitionists lent a hand for women's suffrage, few union men spoke out when women were fired in droves after World War II, male anti-war activists thought nothing of a poster campaign: "Girls say yes to boys who say no," and gay men have been shamefully silent in our Lesbian struggle against breast cancer.

Yes, men have oppressions, but they also have many times our resources for fighting them. Let them do it.

God

━━━➤●◅━━━

In *The Color Purple* by Alice Walker, the novel's protagonist Celie discusses religion with her lover Shug. Shug talks about the omnipresence of images of men, and how easy it is to begin to believe that man is god because of this. She talks about the discipline it takes to get these images out of one's mind and to replace them by conjuring images from nature. Celie comments on the difficulty of doing this: "Everytime I conjure up a rock, I throw it."

What is at stake here for radical feminists is the need to forge a supportive ideology that is not centered on reaction against patriarchy, because conjuring the rock to throw is still a form of worship of the male god.

Changing the pronouns in patriarchal worship, so that Big Daddy Above becomes Big Mama Above may signal some movement toward taking back our power, but if a woman is still locating the source of her power outside herself, she is still internalizing the most disempowering aspects of man-worship—regardless of which pronoun she uses.

Diane Stein explains her concept of goddess worship in *The Women's Spirituality Book*:

> "The goddess is not an out-there force among the far stars or beyond death, but is here and now and living. In philosopher Mary Daly's concept of active creation, she is verb rather than noun and is women's Be-ing. Since the goddess is... within and all around us, the powers of divinity and creation are both individual

and shared... She is the power to make of women's lives what women will. With the tenet, 'Thou art goddess,' freedom of choice is a central issue; women take charge of who they are and what they do, not with blame or guilt, but with responsibility for their actions and choices."

But isn't this the same as having no goddess at all? No! Without a sense of the infinite and divine nature within us and a sense of the interconnectedness of women with nature, a woman may by default find herself reverting to the patriarchal, materialistic, limited and limiting concept of herself as a product of her culture, an isolated being alone with her experience.

The goddess is a wild, liberating concept, and one that can enable us to throw out the old scripts of victimization, depression, self-sabotage, and fear and envy of other women. The goddess gives us ongoing permission to tap into her ancient and sacred fury, her ecstasy—and to break, with wild and lusty acts, what Daly calls the "terrible taboo" of patriarchy—women touching women!

Chastity

"I regard as mortal sin not only the lying evidence of
the senses in matters of love, but also the illusion
which the senses seek to create where love is not
whole or complete. One must love, say I, with all of
one's self — or live a life of utter chastity."

— George Sand

Those two sentences would put a considerable number of
women's therapists out of business. "The lying evidence
of the senses" dispenses with all those relationships
based on sexual attraction, chemistry, and lust. "The illusion which the senses seek to create" clause eliminates
those relationships based on romance. So, what is left?
Well, as she says, chastity. And then that other thing —
that love with "all of one's self."

And what, pray tell, is that — now that we're not allowed
to feel sexual or even romantic? Good question. And the
key lies in the qualifier "with all of one's self." I suspect
that many of us when we love sexually or romantically
are loving with as much of ourselves as we know at the
time. But Sand is implying that there is a self beyond our
body or the current movie of personality in which we are
starring.

And so the focus shifts from finding, attracting, keeping,
fixing a mate to knowing who we are. Not as glamorous,
perhaps, but also not so haphazard. Go to a bar and you
might not meet anyone, but *you* sure as hell will be there.

Women are forever patching love up from the outside,
when it's basically an inside job. You cannot get love until

you feel that you are loved. Say what? Well, but it's true. Feeling unloved is a desperate condition, and there is something so unsexy about desperation. The woman who comes to rescue an unloved woman is coming to rescue, not to love.

I am afraid that George Sand is right.

Orbits

It takes a lot of thrust to break out of an orbit.

This is a good thing to keep in mind when we are engaged in breaking old habits and trying on new behaviors.

Toxic families have gravitational pulls, and so do addictions. And then there are religious beliefs from childhood, habits of constriction from being told one was stupid/clumsy/ugly/untalented, discrimination because one is female, Black, young, old, Puerto Rican, disabled, and so forth. The status quo, by virtue of its mass, exerts an enormous pull on all of us.

But people do break out of their orbits. It's just not easy. And it does take a lot of thrust. During the thrust stage, a woman may become so focused on her own experience that she alienates others with her obsessive drive for justice or freedom. She may deny or censor the experiences and opinions of everyone who is not in perfect agreement. Her rage may burn everyone who tries to touch her, and her temper may be explosive.

She is breaking out of orbit. She is trying to come up with a formula for combustion great enough to challenge the forces of inertia that hold her in orbit. She may not make it. She may burn out before she manages to break away. But she just might find herself heading toward the stars.

When we see a woman who has all that fire, can we learn to stand back, cut her some slack, and wish her well on her journey? Can we ask her to tell us about where she's headed instead of demanding an explanation for all the explosions? And if she makes it, and we resist the urge to pull her back, can we use the example of her thrust to liberate ourselves?

Compromise

―――――――

"Women will gain nothing by a compromising attitude... The woman who possesses love for her sex, for
the world, for truth, justice and right will not hesitate
to place herself upon record as opposed to falsehood,
no matter under what guise of age or holiness it
appears."

—Matilda Joslyn Gage

I named myself after Matilda Gage, in honor of this
fiercely uncompromised Suffrage worker.

We all know about the partnership of Susan B. Anthony
and Elizabeth Cady Stanton in the fight for Women's
Suffrage. But few of us know that this partnership was
actually a "triumverate," with Matilda as the third leader.

She made her first appearance at the Syracuse National
Convention in 1852, where, unknown and unannounced,
she mounted the podium to deliver a paper on what
women throughout history had been able to achieve—at
a time when suffragists were still arguing about what
women might be able to accomplish if given the vote. Her
paper, in the days before Women's Studies, represented
an unprecedented amount of persistent, radical, and solitary scholarship.

She was also there at the trial of Susan B. Anthony, who
had cast a vote to challenge the constitutionality of exclud-
ing women from the ballot. And Matilda edited the paper
of the National Women's Suffrage Association, and she
wrote three chapters of *The History of Women's Suffrage*.

So why was she written out of history? Probably because

of another book she wrote, *Woman, Church and State*. This little book, which is back in print, was an explosive expose of christianity's persecution of women. Reading it, one cannot escape the conclusion that woman-hating is not some unfortunate oversight or temporary footnote in the history of the church, but that it is, in fact, the underlying rationale. According to Dale Spender (*Women of Ideas And What Men Have Done to Them*), Matilda asserts that christianity is only meaningful when women are oppressed.

She also spoke out about rape and the non-conviction of rapists, about the double standard applied to prostitution, about the oppression of Native Americans, about women in prison, about pay equity.

Matilda never made concessions to the times in which she was living. For her, loving women was all of a piece. You could not make excuses or apologies for the institutions that were oppressing women, no matter how entrenched they were, even in the minds and lives of women. Her radicalism, however, was alienating the Women's Christian Temperance Union, and she was eventually manipulated out of her own movement by the very women she had the most reason to trust. The betrayal by both Stanton and Anthony was devastating.

But history has vindicated Matilda Joslyn Gage, and her work—referred to as "logical and fearless" in her day, still holds up with the timelessness of uncompromised truth.

Power

"You see, we *have* power. Men have to dream to get power from the spirits and they think of everything they can—song and speeches and marching around, hoping that the spirits will notice them and give them some power. But we *have* power..."

— Marie Chona

Marie Chona was a Papago Indian woman, described as a "great leader among women." Born in 1845, she narrated her autobiography in 1935 at the age of ninety.

Among her people, the greatest gift and power was that of creating songs, either through medicine power or through dreams. Marie had that gift from the time she was a small child, even though she was not able to go into the desert like her brother, because, as a female child, she had to work.

Marie married a medicine man, but when he took a second wife, she left him and returned to her family — an unusual action for a married woman to take. She remarried another medicine man, a man much older than herself, and, according to her narration, this was a painful event. It was through this marriage, however, she was able to acquire the knowledge that led to her becoming a tribal matriarch.

Marie chafed against the restrictions for women, but by defying, subverting, and appropriating where she could, she was able to prevail and live her dream of being a healer.

At the time when she was dictating her autobiography,

she was asked if she was satisfied with her life. Marie answered that she was or else she would have done something about it.

Old Age

"I think even lying on my bed I can still do something."
—Dorothea Dix

Dorothea made this statement lying on her bed at the age of eighty-five. Throughout her life she had fought a long, hard battle to reform conditions for the developmentally disabled and the emotionally disturbed. She never retired. She never gave up. She never "passed the torch."

I remember reading in the autobiography of Martha Graham about how the board of directors of her own dance company had retired her against her will. She went on to form another company and keep working. Later, when she was in the hospital with a stroke, she was visited by a therapist who was going to help her adjust to her new life, a life without dancing. Martha told the woman that, although she respected the therapist's good intentions, all her life she had relied on her body, and she was just going to have to continue doing that. And she did recover to work again.

Old age is a fact of life. Denial of it is not empowering. Ignorance of the changes in our bodies is not empowering. But neither is ignorance about the many aggressive attitudes toward aging that masquerade as facts, when they are nothing of the sort. Often changes in lifestyle or interests are attributed to aging, when in fact women at all ages make radical changes in our lives.

A woman may decide to quit dancing at twenty-five or at sixty-five. She may also decide not to quit. Dorothea could have decided to retire from her activism.

116

Obviously, she chose not to.

Challenge the mandates of aging. Challenge them intelligently, but challenge them nonetheless.

Borrowing

"It was impossible, however, to find an English equiv-
alent word that would combine all the reasons for
which the club was formed... The name would have
to stand for independence, educational and progressive. We finally decided to take a Chinese word
[jeleab], and, by using it, Anglicize it."

—Clara Lee

In 1913, Clara Lee founded the Chinese Women's Jeleab
Association in San Francisco. This was an organization
modeled after the anglo-american women's club movement, but incorporating a pride in Chinese nationalism
inspired by the recent revolution.

Clara Lee and the women in her organization were not
interested in assimilation, nor were they interested in
returning to the traditional role of the Chinese woman.
They wanted to incorporate the best of both worlds—but
to do so, they had to challenge the deficiencies in both.

It is interesting to note that where the Chinese culture
lacked a model for women's self-improvement organizations, the English language lacked a word for independence that was inclusive of ideas of education and social
change. In the one culture, the rights of the individual
were subordinated to the its institutions, whereas, in the
other, a fanatic ideology of individualism had resulted in
a restrictive language. It took the "jeleab" of Clara Lee
and her fellow club members to forge a synthesis for
themselves.

In a culture of disposable commodities, it's easy to

become a bridge-burner, but we all need our roots—desperately. The fact that most of us have been transplanted, literally or figuratively, makes our need for healthy roots even more imperative.

Salvaging, although nowhere near as flamboyant as torching bridges, is a far more radical act. In fact, if the whole point of bridge-burning is to discourage retreat, salvaging is a much more effective deterrent, because we have taken all the good parts of our previous experience with us. What's to look back at?

Security

"Security is an illusion."

— Jean Mountaingrove

Jean Mountaingrove lives up in the hills of Southern Oregon. She lives very simply, without electricity and with water supplied by a gravity-flow system. For ten years she published *Womanspirit*, the first magazine of women's spirituality, from her home. Jean has lived on the land and in Lesbian community for many years, and just as her home, Rootworks, is the repository of a quarter-century of Lesbian books and journals, so Jean herself is a repository for several generations of Lesbian wisdom.

If Jean is right, that security is just an illusion, does that mean we're all condemned to lifetimes of uncertainty and constant anxiety?

This question reminds me of a friend who was watching birds migrating south. She said, "There! If I was one of those birds, I would be a nervous wreck, trying to keep up with the others, petrified that they were going to leave me behind, because they all know where they're going and I don't — and worrying myself sick about where we were going to spend the night!" She was only partially joking.

My friend is an example of someone whose symbols for security are so illusory, they virtually preclude her having any peace of mind at all. Fortunately for birds, they are more trusting of their instincts.

Can we get back to that innate trust — that sense of oneness with our being and our environment, or have we created such a monstrously artificial habitat for ourselves that our well-being is now dependent on money, pensions, health insurance, and so forth? Is it too late?

Maybe for that world it is. But I think of Jean, growing her own food, using her solar shower, working on her writing and her art projects, and participating as a vital member of her Lesbian community. She lives so simply and so marginally by patriarchal standards — and yet, she is one of the most secure people I know. She understands both her nature and her place, and she lives true to both.

Ironically, it seems that in understanding security to be an illusion, Jean has found a measure of security.

Theatre People

"Barbarians have swept down through the ages of all civilizations, wielding fire and sword... They destroyed cities and monuments and works of art and miracles of engineering; but they knew that in order to conquer they had to destroy language; and that was much harder. Occasionally they did it, but not often. Language is the hardest thing of all to annihilate from without. But it can be destroyed from within, and there is a host of barbarians in our midst busily doing it... But you, the theatre people, will be the guardians of language."

—Margaret Webster

Margaret Webster was a Lesbian director and performer. Her mother, Dame May Whitty, had been a great star of the British stage. In 1946, Margaret teamed up with Lesbians Eva Le Gallienne and Cheryl Crawford to open the American Repertory Theatre, a theatre that made history with outstanding productions at popular prices.

I include this quotation as a tribute to my own vocation as a playwright. Electronic media is about moving image. It is not an evolutionary advance over live theatre, nor is it a substitute or replacement for it. It is, pure and simple, an entirely different medium.

Live theatre is about the spoken word. It engages a different set of imaginative faculties and perceptions. It can be the guardian of language, but only if it takes that role seriously. When it tries to compete with what electronic media does (a competition it can never win), the theatre loses that which sets it apart, the very touchstone of its dynamism.

When language loses its specificity, when it loses its poetry, its color — when it sinks to the level of lowest common denominator of human communication, thought becomes truncated also. And as our range of expression becomes more and more limited, so does our range for experiencing and interpreting the world. And the culture, instead of becoming expansive, begins to collapse in on itself.

Live theatre is vital to culture, and this is especially true for Lesbian and feminist cultures that are so censored and distorted by the malestream entertainment industries.

Unfortunately, live theatre is labor intensive and its end product is ephemeral. To produce a play these days is almost an act of faith.

Perhaps we should embrace that as an asset, instead of writing it off as a liability. What if live theatre were once again to be regarded as a sacred art? Changing our concepts of the function of theatre and cherishing its ability to create change at the deepest levels of the psyche, maybe we can begin a revolution in our communities — a movement away from canned cultural products and toward a celebration of ourselves—alive, known to one another and yet transformed, in real time and space and therefore in control of time and space—and, finally, *speaking*.

Loneliness

"The strongest is the loneliest, and the loneliest is the strongest."

—Eleanora Duse

Strength breeds strength. The strong woman has the resources to take a stand, and in taking that stand, she will become even stronger. And the stronger she grows, the more she will become separated from the interests and goals of weaker women. She will become a threat to them. If she does not withdraw to create a protective distance, she will be pushed away. And she will be lonely.

And that is how the strongest becomes the loneliest.

The lonely woman is a woman who has learned early to take comfort in communion with herself. Perhaps through abusive conditioning, she has been taught that she is different, unlovable. To be safe, she keeps to herself. In doing so, she cultivates the riches of her own imagination, and she lives a life not influenced by peer pressure, by trends and fads, by competitive interests. She travels to a different drum.

And in her difference, she will be mocked, scorned, and finally, deserted. If she does not learn to conform, and if she does not cave in emotionally, she will become strong in her aloneness. She will lean on the strength of her convictions; she will defend her vision; she will not be tempted to abandon herself for the approval of others.

And that is how the loneliest becomes the strongest.

Naming

"My silences had not protected me. Your silence will not protect you."

—Audre Lorde

Silence never protects anybody. Naming is power, and the power to name our experience is still very recent for women.

Men have named us: "frigid" instead of "Lesbian," "crazy" instead of "resisting domination," "feminine" instead of "brainwashed," "of limited intelligence [agility, artistic ability, ambition, and so on]" instead of "politically and historically deprived of educational, athletic, political, and cultural opportunities," "man-hating" instead of "truth-telling."

It has only been in the last two decades that there have been words for "date rape," "marital rape," "sexual harassment," and "battered women's syndrome." Our silence on these issues has been interpreted historically to mean that we were enjoying sexual violation, that the references to our bodies and the pressure on us to be sexual were all part of being female—maybe even a compliment or a testimony to our power over men, and that when we finally couldn't take any more, we were criminals.

Are there conditions currently in our lives for which we have still not found a name? And if we have not found a name, are we unconsciously allowing the patriarchy to name it for us, in terms that validate our subjugation?

Take a look at the ways in which you feel bad about yourself. "Too fat," "too thin," "too old," "not good looking?"

Try naming the problem as having been systematically brainwashed by the colonial government to conform to an unrealistic standard, a standard specifically designed to prevent women's identification with one another, to enforce race and class divisions, and to prevent radical action by diverting our energy into obsessive self-hating thoughts and compulsive non-productive activities. Now, haven't you got a better handle on the problem than dieting?

Renaming is critical to the safety and protection of children. Many children are living the experience of being held hostage by terrorists, or of being tortured as prisoners-of-war by the enemy. But children do not have the power to name their experience. Their torturers and enemies are protected by the patriarchal naming of "parents," "mother," "father," "brother"—in other words, "family." And the use of that word prevents the kind of radical action that would be imperative if children owned the power of naming.

How can a brainwashed caste reclaim the power to name? We begin with our feelings. We begin by knowing there is a reason, a good reason, for what we are feeling. And then we go looking for that reason, in the past or in the present. And we recruit other women in our search for the reason. What did they see? What did they experience? *And what shall we call it?*

Class

"Class consciousness is knowing which side of the fence you're on. Class analysis is figuring out who is there with you."
—from a poster published by Press Gang

Lesbian-feminist author Julia Penelope edited an anthology called *Out of the Class Closet: Lesbians Speak*. In it, Lesbian after Lesbian wrote about her confusion about class. Most of the contributors felt they could not identify themselves wholly as a member of any class. Some had been poor, but had become middle class in terms of income. Others had been raised middle class, but were now poor. Does class refer to having had braces as a child, or does it refer to educational background? And can class be equated with privilege in reference to women, who are frequently second-class citizens in the patriarchal household? Does class privilege translate automatically to enfranchisement when a middle class child has been raised in terror and with sexual abuse?

Many women find ourselves on different sides of the fence in different circumstances, and this makes for very dicey alliances across class lines. Skin privilege, heterosexual privilege, age privilege, able-bodied privilege—all of these translate to class privilege. And, conversely, class privilege can serve to neutralize the stigma of prejudice.

How can we maintain solidarity across class lines when these divisions are so omnipresent and such tangible and painful reminders of the gross inequalities of the system? And how real is that solidarity when middle and upper class "sisters" in seeming coalition with poor women have no intention of surrendering what privilege they have managed to wrest from the system? How real is that solidarity when the acceptance of this inequality renders such coalitions exercises in low self-esteem and disenfranchisement for poverty-class women? Is the "diversity" model appropriate for class difference?

The fences of class seem to constitute a maximum security prison, no escape. Mobility, maybe — but escape? Never.

What we can do is begin, within the walls of this prison, to construct other systems that do not replicate or reinforce these divisions. We begin wherever we can. We begin in our thoughts, in our one-on-one interactions, in our choices about how we will use what privilege we have. We begin by talking about it. We begin with awareness. We begin sometimes by picking our own organization to pieces and starting all over. We begin by challenging our goals if we exploit class privilege to achieve them. We begin over and over and over. We begin by listening, by hearing our grief, our rage, our arrogance, our ignorance, our brainwashing.

And beginning is no small thing.

Dissatisfaction

"Remember, the grateful prisoner may get extra rations, but it's the indignant one who gets over the wall."

—Carolyn Gage

This is my own quotation from *Take Stage!*, a book I wrote about my Lesbian theatre experiences. Gloria Steinem has used the phrase "terminally grateful" to describe women, and I have found this can be especially applicable to Lesbians. Not because we have an innate character flaw, but because we have been subjected to centuries of horrific oppression. We have reason to feel astonished that we are still alive, overwhelmed with awe that our presence is tolerated.

But we have a radical imperative to challenge these attitudes. And this isn't easy. The woman tickled to death that the glass is half full is a lot more fun to be around than the woman who is forever reminding us that it is half empty, even as she dies of dehydration from refusing to drink it.

And then, of course, there is all the emphasis on gratitude in the traditional recovery programs. Gratitude has its place. Maybe if I was a white, anglo, male, christian heterosexual, I would know what that is, but I'm not and I don't.

Focus is focus, and how can a woman give her attention to adjusting to a situation, and at the same time be planning her escape from it? Adjustment and liberation are mutually exclusive goals. Occasionally, a truly brilliant escape artist will "pass" as a well-adjusted (grateful) prisoner, as a cover for her subversive activities—but she never makes the mistake of believing her own propaganda.

Dissatisfaction may seem pessimistic, but in my experience, it gives evidence of a deep optimism, a faith that there is a "somewhere else" and that it will be possible to get there in this lifetime.

Brothers

"... in the history of human affections... the least satisfying is the fraternal. Brothers are to sisters what sisters can never be to brothers as objects of engrossing and devoted affection."*

—Harriet Martineau

Of course, British author and social critic Harriet Martineau was writing about relations among anglo-europeans in the nineteenth century, when women were not allowed to inherit property, vote, attend college, earn a decent living, own their own wages or children, and so forth. They had to content themselves with living vicariously through their brothers, or, at worst, becoming ingratiating to them, because often the brothers would have complete control over their sisters' finances later in life, acting as if they had a right to their inheritance while their sisters were charity cases.

Times have changed, but vestiges of this legacy are still ingrained in many families.

As women begin to remember and share stories of their sexual abuse, another alarming facet of "fraternity" is coming to light. Many, many girls have been sexually and/or emotionally abused by their brothers, and this abuse was tacitly supported by the family. I remember how my brother, who was unable to endure being alone, would invade my privacy any time he pleased, interrupting whatever I was doing, and frequently destroying whatever project I was engaged in. My appeals for intervention were ignored, because my brother was, after all, the young lord of the family, and what could I possibly have to do that was more important than meeting his needs? This was crucial training for my future role as a female in a man's world.

Patriarchy begins at home, and although the presence of a patriarchal tyrant is usually the primary source of oppression, it is in the relations between brothers and sisters that the lessons of inequality are most painfully brought home.

Metaphors

———◇———

"We must work with the metaphor in which we find ourselves."

—Matricia

Matricia is a spiritual healer, and a very effective one. This quotation sums up her methodology, which has implications for the radical feminist.

Although Matricia founds her practice on a bedrock of faith in the individual's spiritual perfection, she takes the manifestations of disease very, very seriously. It is the metaphor with which she works.

The radical activist is a form of spiritual healer also. She has to be, because there is insufficient evidence in the record of human relations to warrant any belief that people are capable — or even desirous — of enlightened self-government. Where do we get our vision, if not from some intuitive knowledge that there is more to life than what appears on the surface? The fact that women who have experienced the least justice in their lives are the most passionate questers for it, would certainly point to an experience gained on some other plane — whether from books, or imagination, or past lives, or a simultaneous spiritual reality.

What if the circumstances of our current world do represent metaphors? Does that imply we don't need to take them seriously? On the contrary, if this were true, we would find ourselves with more, not less responsibility, because we are responsible for the symbols we use to express ourselves. As feminists, we understand very well how control of vocabulary can shape perceptions and experiences. In that arena, we have taken it upon ourselves to invent our own words. But what about the more concrete symbols, the solid convictions of a patriarchal world gone mad? How on earth can we deal with them as metaphors?

The first step might be to examine the substance behind our symbols: Boys will be boys; competition is the natural law; survival of the fittest is the natural order; it's every woman for herself. Can we grasp a different order and tear our eyes away from our oppression long enough to establish in mind the certainty of another kind of law, a spiritual law? What would a world look like where another's good was enriching to me, where boys did not have to be boys, where cooperation was the law of nature? When we do not challenge our fundamental assumptions about reality, we often end up with interchangeable metaphors. How often has one oppressive regime been toppled, only to be replaced by another?

When I hit a brick wall with activism, I turn back to these words of Matricia and take some time out from the struggle to wrestle with my metaphors. The change in perspective is always invigorating and frequently provides the key to more effective action.

Passing

"But the reality is that there is no privilege in a life
that is a lie... The lie is always in the way, the lie
always obscures intimacy and possibility."

—Victoria Brownworth

Lesbian journalist and activist Victoria Brownworth was
writing about her parents' destructive myths about their
social status, the lie of "genteel poverty" that distanced
them from their neighbors.

If passing does prevent intimacy and doesn't bring privilege, then why do so many people do it? Because it creates the *illusion* of belonging.

So many of us grew up believing that life was really happening somewhere else, that the "real" people were over
there, busy being rich, or light-skinned, or male, or col-
lege-educated. The more we could make ourselves look
or talk like them, the closer we were coming to that myth-
ical place of "having arrived."

And there is not only the pull toward what we perceive
as privilege, but the push away from family shame and
whatever symbols or insignia we consider to be dead
giveaways: the "wrong" neighborhood, the old car, the
"bad" hair, the "incorrect" grammar. These facts of life
may have become freighted with negative values in families desperate to displace shame onto things outside the
self: Poverty equals failure, lack of conformity to white,
middle-class, youth-oriented standards of beauty equals
ugliness, lack of education equals stupidity, failure to
achieve recognition equals lack of worth. And truly, it is

valid to flee failure, ugliness, stupidity, and lack of worth. These are terrifying curses.

The problem is that these qualities refer to deficiencies in our self-esteem, distortions in the way we see ourselves —not in our external, imposed, or arbitrary circumstances. Giving this kind of life-and-death power to the outside world is a fatal strategy, because even if we can manage to "arrive" on these terms, our struggle to retain our foothold in this slippery world will remain a desperate one. Acquisition is not the same as claiming qualities as part of our intrinsic nature.

So many, many lives are wasted in the pursuit of worthless goals! Our indoctrination by school systems whose primary purpose is to teach fear of outside authority, does not aid us in critical thinking. The radical feminist must daily put herself back at the center of her reality, must make her highest understanding the perpetual standard for evaluating who she is and how she locates herself in relation to others.

It is a chiropractic of the soul, and the frequency of adjustments should be proportionate to the distortions we encounter in our thinking.

Refusing to Compromise

"I'd rather go down in history as one lone Negro who dared to tell the government that it had done a dastardly thing than to save my skin by taking back what I have said. I would consider it an honor to spend whatever years are necessary in prison as the one member of the race who protested, rather than be with all the 11,999,999 Negroes who didn't have to go to prison because they kept their mouths shut."

—Ida B. Wells-Barnett

Ida Wells-Barnett was being threatened by the United States government with charges of treason when she made this declaration. In 1917, she had launched a campaign to draw the public's attention to the government's hanging of twelve members of an African American regiment that had been involved in a race riot in Texas. She had distributed buttons and called for a national day of mourning for the martyred soldiers. With the mobilization for World War I going on, her indictment of the military as racist—indeed, as the enemy of African Americans!—was seen as divisive and unpatriotic. As with her anti-lynching campaigns, there were many African Americans unwilling to stand with her in the fight.

Ida had also protested the exclusion of African Americans from the great Columbian Exposition of 1893, distributing to fair-goers ten thousand pamphlets titled *The Reason Why the Colored American Is Not Represented in the World's Columbian Exposition*. When the Exposition board planned a belated "Colored Jubilee Day," replete with 2000 watermelons, Ida boycotted the event.

Frederick Douglass, on the other hand, had participated

in the fair as a representative of Haiti! He also supported and attended the Jubilee.

She protested showings of the racist film *Birth of a Nation*, exposed the segregationalist policies of the YMCA, and finally resigned from the Afro-American Council in protest of Booker T. Washington's policies of appeasement.

Distressed with the lack of a written record of African American history, she wrote her own, *Crusade for Justice*. She died just before its completion in 1931. The book was not published until 1970, forty years later.

Interestingly, Ida's activism was set in motion by an incident similar to that experienced by Rosa Parks. She had boarded the ladies' coach of a train on the way to a teaching job. The conductor, denying first class seats to African Americans, asked her to move to the smoking car. She refused and was forcibly removed. At the next stop, she returned to Memphis and filed suit. She won, but the Tennessee Supreme Court reversed the decision, claiming that her actions had been prompted by a desire to cause trouble.

She later wrote that she had "firmly believed all along that the law was on our side and would, when we appealed to it, give us justice. I [felt] shorn of that belief and utterly discouraged."

But out of her profound disillusionment with the system, was born her militant activism and her uncompromising attitude toward racism.

Critics

"To note an artist's limitations is but to define his [sic] talent."

—Willa Cather

"Criticism? Horrors! I never read the reviews!" How many of us say that?

Well, here's a story: The nineteenth-century Lesbian actor Charlotte Cushman began her career as an opera singer. Her first (and last) season in New Orleans was a disaster. Only eighteen and a natural contralto, she was hopelessly miscast in soprano roles — and the critics were merciless. Stranded hundreds of miles from home, Charlotte had no alternative but to play out the contract. Night after night, she was booed from the stage, and there was no let-up in the scathing reviews.

Finally, one of her critics suggested in his notice that she might do better if she confined herself to speaking roles. Although the remark was probably intended facetiously, Charlotte chose to take it as an endorsement of her potential. She presented the notice to the head of the company. He, being tied to her contract, was as eager as she to find a way out. Charlotte was cast as Lady Macbeth and the rest is history.

Another actor might have stopped reading the reviews weeks earlier and decided that her critics were her enemies. Charlotte, however, had not done that. She had paid attention — not to their panning of her, because she already knew she was out of her depth musically — but to what insights the critics might be able to offer, even if it meant reading between the lines. And Charlotte was wise enough to see that in defining her limitations, they might actually be helpful in defining her talent.

Incest

"We must say to every member of our society: If you violate your children, they may not speak today, but as we gather our strength and stand beside them, they will, one day, speak your name. They will speak every single name."

—Marilyn Van Derbur

Confronting. Naming. What a burden for the survivor of abuse, the incest survivor, the rape victim! We have already been victimized. It's happened. We have gotten through it. We are coping. Don't tell us that we are expected to go back into the burning building and relive the trauma all over again—in family gatherings, in court -rooms, in meetings with bosses or supervisors or school boards. Don't tell us we are expected to draw more atten- tion to our case, experience more invasion of privacy, open our private lives to more adversarial scrutiny, invite more alienation and ostracization, draw more headlines, face more bureaucratic men, subject ourselves to more charges of lying, blaming, "false memory syndrome," or indulging in pathological fantasies. If we're supposed to be taking care of ourselves, how could we be expected to put ourselves through the ordeal of telling?

Good question. And not one easily answered. Sometimes it's a question of time. Sometimes the time is never. Sometimes it's a question of support. Sometimes all the support in the world can't shield the victim from her worst nightmares.

Why tell? Because it may bring the perpetrator to justice. It may slow them down. It may alert others to the risks of contact with this person. It may result in financial reparations. It may—but don't count on it—bring about a change of heart.

But more to the point, it may be a step in the healing process. It may be the final act of self-validation—that even in the face of skepticism or scapegoating or threats, the victim refuses to be silent. It may be the speaking/hearing-into-being which is most needed in the recovery of self-esteem. It may be a political act that enlarges the scope of the incident from a personal accident to an act of war. It may be the action needed to put the victim in touch with a larger sense of community.

When I am feeling too weary to confront one more situation, I remember the army of anonymous women who came before me and confronted: the women who heard themselves called whores in their rape trials, the women who were locked up in mental institutions for telling the truth about their brothers or fathers, the women who had horse shit thrown on them for wearing bloomers, the Chinese women who were murdered for cutting their hair and unbinding their feet—the army of women who told and lived the truth at all costs. And I know that most of the freedoms I have today are because of these women.

For there to be widespread social change, a critical mass of protest needs to be reached. That mass is not reached when women wait to see who else will come forward, or when we wait until it's safe. It is reached when women come forward and come forward and come forward, in season and out of season, alone or in groups. It is reached when individual woman after individual woman determines in her heart that she cannot remain silent—no matter what.

Exhaustion

It was Anne Morrow Lindbergh who pointed out that being insincere was the most exhausting thing in life.

The radical feminist, in her haste to repudiate the artificial roles for women and the toxic teachings of patriarchy, may end by trading one form of insincerity for another.

We are very complex creatures, we women, and our lives are filled with contradictions. Although many of our tastes and habits and rituals have been conditioned by consumerism, sexism, homophobia, and so forth, these same tastes and habits and rituals can represent personal symbols and metaphors for positive and affirming qualities. Sometimes in our rigorous anti-patriarchal housecleaning, we can throw the baby out with the bath water. And we can also do violence to the personal symbologies of others.

Sometimes the religion of one's childhood is so replete with deep spiritual connections and private meaning, it does violence to one's being to repudiate it wholesale on political grounds, without taking into account the ways in which an individual may have appropriated or subverted the teaching.

Sometimes our political consciousness can outstrip our emotional needs for grounding in tradition, for the comfort of the familiar, or for the uncritiqued joys of indulging in frivolity.

I am reminded of the experiences of children of radical utopians. As a child, Louisa May Alcott was taken to live at Fruitlands, where her father was attempting to find the way to perfect diet and natural living. He did a lot of theorizing, while his wife and children suffered considerably. At one point, no one was allowed to eat anything except apples. While Bronson Alcott was experiencing an invigorating renunciation of what were for him corrupt symbols, his children were experiencing punitive deprivation.

When we find ourselves exhausted and burned out, it might be a good time to do a "sincerity check." Are we being sincere about the multiplicity of our needs as complex beings? Are we denying our need for more connection with our past, for more out-and-out fun? Are we imposing military rule over ourselves? What if those who share our ideology are not necessarily the zany and spontaneous folks we thrive on being around?

Children have boundless energy, and I'm not so sure that our subsequent loss of energy is a function of aging. Could it be the result of banishment?

Old People

"The thinking powers of old people are strong
and if one of them thinks good things for you,
whatever he [sic] wishes for you, you will
obtain that good fortune."

—Mountain Wolf Woman

These are the words of Mountain Wolf Woman, a First Nation Winnebago woman born in 1884 in Wisconsin. The Winnebagos had been subjected to many forced migrations by the United States government: first from the Green Bay area to southern Wisconsin, then to northeastern Iowa, then to north-central Minnesota, then southern Minnesota, then the Dakota Territory. This last move was so disastrous, resulting in starvation, that the Winnebago leaders negotiated a move on their own behalf, appealing to the First Nation Omahas in Nebraska. It is a cruel joke that this tribe came to be known as the "wandering Winnebagos," and that their tribal name has been appropriated as a trade mark for mobile homes.

Mountain Wolf Woman, aware of this history, stressed the importance of respecting the elders in her autobiography. And her reason goes beyond the usual sense of duty or decency. She states that old people have power.

In a materialist culture, old age is seen as decline—the downslope of a linear evolution that reached its peak during young adulthood. But life process can be viewed as a spiritual evolution in which the fascination with symbols gives way progressively to engagement with the substance behind the symbol.

145

Experience has a way of teaching the advantages of shape-shifting over the tedious mechanics of forcing events. Mountain Wolf Woman acknowledges this different perspective on aging in her tribute to the "thinking powers" of old people.

This is not to say that there are not old people with corrupt thinking, whose advanced years have only led to entrenchment of prejudice. But in a rush not to appear ageist, there is a danger in minimalizing the very real value of experience accrued through more than a half century of living.

Mountain Wolf Woman goes further to imply that these elders have the ability to shape-shift in favor of those they would bless. We certainly are aware how we have been limited and conditioned by the toxic ideas of our forebears. Why couldn't we also receive empowerment and momentum from our mentors?

Image

"The WSPU must not only be strong; it must not only be independent; it must not only be uncompromising. It must also APPEAR to be strong, it must APPEAR to be independent, it must APPEAR to be uncompromising."

—Christabel Pankhurst

Christabel, a leader of the suffragist movement in England, was writing about the Women's Social and Political Union at the time when the WSPU had adopted a policy of militant activism.

The sentiment in the quotation seems self-evident. What is the point of being strong, and independent if you are going to appear weak? And yet many of us continually catch ourselves doing just that.

I find that, especially among sister Lesbians, I am tempted to act less educated than I am, to downplay the force of my opinions, to dismiss my own accomplishments, to appear unsure of things I am sure about, to pretend that my opinion of myself is based on the assessment of others, to act as if I need help or advice when in fact I don't at all. What confused behavior! What mixed messages!

What's going on, when a strong woman feels it necessary to act weak?

Well, as a radical feminist, my first analysis is the political one. Are the penalties real or imaginary for a woman who owns her work and knows her worth?

We all know what men have done to uppity women. In

the past they burned us. In the last century, they denied us access to resources. In the early part of this century, they incarcerated us. Today, according to Mary Daly, the witch-burnings take the form of tokenizing us.

But what about women? What do women do to uppity women? Historically we shunned and trashed one another. The woman who owned her body was perverted or promiscuous. The woman who aspired to an intellectual life was a bad mother. The woman with her eye on financial independence was accused of being mercenary.

Have things really changed? I have been trashed and shunned, sometimes by whole communities. So have all the other radical feminists I know. Our crimes? Being a little too big for our britches. Wanting a little more than what has been allotted to us. Daring to speak our minds without catering to popular opinion. *Being less damaged.*

So, should a woman disguise her strength? No, but she needs to draw *very* clear boundaries between her personal and her public life. She also needs to draw a clear boundary between her real friends—those whose opinions will matter to her—and her casual friends and acquaintances, whose opinions should not affect her peace of mind or sense of herself.

Freedom

"I saw a woman sleeping. In her sleep, she dreamt life stood before her, and held in each hand a gift—in the one hand love, in the other freedom. And she said to the woman, "Choose." And the woman waited long: and she said, "Freedom." And life said "Thou hast well chosen. If thou hadst said 'Love' I would have given thee that thou didst ask for; and I would have gone from thee, and returned to thee no more. Now the day will come when I shall return. In that day I shall bear both gifts in one hand." I heard the woman laugh in her sleep."

—Olive Schreiner

Passion

———⇒❖⇐———

> "I think our culture doesn't recognize passion, because real passion has the power to disrupt boundaries."
>
> —bell hooks

How many times are women shamed for coloring outside the lines! And do we stop to ask "Whose lines?" and "Whose picture?"

How many family gatherings, academic settings, corporate meetings are structured to penalize the woman who dares to respond authentically to the core issues behind "business as usual?" And how many times do women hold our rage, our shock, our grief in check for fear of appearing out of control, somewhat less than adult, "unprofessional?" I think of Rosa Parks stubbornly refusing to budge from her seat while all the busy folks were just trying to get where they were going. Couldn't she see that they had nothing to do with her issues—that inconveniencing them was projecting her anger onto the wrong target? Didn't she realize the futility of one woman taking a stand against a time-honored institution? And yet Rosa's passionate defiance triggered a boycott of all the buses in Atlanta and brought the smouldering issues of racial injustice into the open where everyone had to confront them.

The bravest and most significant actions I have ever taken were always accompanied by warnings from an internal voice telling me that I was being selfish, inconsiderate, inappropriate, immature. Always. My own boundary police are infinitely more vigilant than any from the outside world. The woman who is waiting for a

150

venue that will be receptive to her passions and her spontaneity will spend her life stifling her humanity—or she will spend a fortune seeking out therapeutic situations where she can express herself freely, but completely outside the forums where this expression could effect social change.

Passion moves things. It may be met by an immediate backlash of shame and ridicule, but it does move things. Nothing is ever the same after an outburst of passion. Oh, people will try to pretend it is, but it's not. You may never know the full effect of your passion, but it is always an act of power—and the more the world screams that you have done nothing but make a fool of yourself, the more you can know you made a difference.

The Bag Lady Syndrome

" ... the Nightmare took variant forms. In its most drastic form the plot was something like this: I do not yet have my B.A. I am quite elderly... and I am attending night school attempting to obtain this degree. I am in a large auditorium-like classroom, seated near the back, taking notes in order to pass the course. I am wearing a dowdy kind of dress and am feeling quite confused and addle-brained."

—Mary Daly

This is the nightmare of a Lesbian with three doctoral degrees. She goes on to elaborate:

"The message is clear. I never really did get any of those degrees. A woman could not get them. A woman could not be legitimated by patriarchy's institutions of higher education. Doctor Mary Daly does not exist. I am an Imposter."

I remember sitting in a meeting with several women, all of whom appeared to be successful and secure in their lives. Somehow we got on the subject of money. I began to express my fears that I could not support myself, although I had been doing so since I was nineteen. I told these women how my financial independence had always seemed anomalous, the result of some accident instead of my hard work. Deep down, I have a vision of myself being unable to survive, homeless, and on the streets.

To my great surprise every one of the women present expressed exactly the same fear. I couldn't believe it.

What is it about this archetypal bag-lady image? Why are so many of us haunted by her specter, when there is seemingly nothing in our lives to indicate we will end up like her?

Mary Daly has explained it: Our achievements under patriarchy *are* anomalous. We are not supposed to be independent, educated, satisfied with ourselves, owning our own work. Even three doctorates will not be enough to prove we are educated. The woman down to ninety pounds must still feel she weighs too much. The woman who has built her own home, started her own business, achieved her own goals, must still question her competency.

Patriarchy follows the lives of women with a big eraser. We can try to outrun it. We can sell out, doing the kind of work patriarchy will perpetuate. Or we can live and work such that our achievements will be cherished and recorded by women. We can give up, finally and forever, all hope of validation from patriarchy. We can begin to learn to celebrate ourselves and one another. And then, when the spectral bag lady comes wheeling her shopping cart across our field of dreams, instead of fleeing in terror, we can load her up with goodies.

In her autobiography, *Outercourse*, Mary narrates an episode where she was being introduced along with other members of the faculty by a good old boy. Everyone else was "Doctor." Mary, of course, was "Miss Daly."

Three degrees were not enough.

Time

"We only have about half-an-hour.
 Let's do what we can."

—Charlotte Mew

These were words written by the Lesbian poet Charlotte Mew to her new friend and patron "Mrs. Sappho" (Catherine Dawson Scott), in reference to the amount of time we have on this earth.

And yet Charlotte Mew ended up shortening her "half-an-hour," committing suicide at the age of fifty-nine.

Time. Not enough to achieve the great things we want to do, and yet too many days of pain, of frustration, or loneliness. Living in the future, living in the past. How to get to the "now?" And why bother, if "now" is not so pretty?

What is the radical orientation to time? Well, my opinion is in the title of this book: *Like There's No Tomorrow*. Live as if today is all you have, that's not to say live hedonistically, in frantic denial, or with over-heated distraction. It is to say, live right now at the most radical level of what you envision as ideal. This means to live with integrity, to live without betraying another woman—even if you can, even if you think she deserves it, even if she'll never know. It means to live as if you were free at the center of your soul—to treat other women with benevolence, forbearance, compassion as if you were safe, loved, secure, and immensely powerful.

And this takes a whopping amount of spiritual discipline and imagination in the face of scarcity, fear, and dog-eat-dog. But it can be done, and, truly, there will be no tomorrow unless we learn to live this way. It has been my experience that living like this will attract the other women who are doing this—and you will find yourself in the company of such amazons as will take your breath away!

Living like there's no tomorrow takes the pressure out of time, takes the stigma out of aging, and the sting out of yesterday.

Laziness

———————

Birth control pioneer Margaret Sanger once referred to laziness as a right that women wanted.

What she was talking about was the right for women to practice birth control—in other words, not to have to have a baby every year of their lives up until menopause or death, whichever came first.

But there is a larger principle involved. What is "laziness," and who defines it? I have heard women refer to reading a book as "doing nothing." Now, as a writer, this is pretty hard to hear. I have also heard women who run themselves ragged with full-time work and raising children, refer to their lives as "not really doing anything." There seems to be some kind of patriarchal catch-22 going on here.

Just what is the organism designed for anyway? And bear in mind that species evolve very, very slowly. It takes thousands and thousands of years for them to make even a minor adjustment to their environment. Then consider the horrendous evolutionary forced march patriarchy has put us through in just the last hundred years:

We no longer eat fresh food. In some cases, it's not even real food. We no longer breath fresh air. We no longer drink pure water. We live in communities no longer bounded by walking distances. We "visit" one another via electronic transmission, radically altering the human context of the communication. (We don't see each other, we don't feel one another's presence, we don't touch.) We experience our culture through patterns of electronically transmitted dots that our brains sort into pictures. We work forty hours a week. And "being productive" is equated with self-esteem.

This is supposed to be an advance over so-called primitive living. And yet, consider that in some tribal societies, the average amount of work done to survive was about fifteen hours a week. The rest of the time was spent in recreation, socializing, creation of culture, spiritual activity. Goods of any real value were all perishable, so there was no such thing as the amassing of capital, and no one owned the land. To live for the sake of living was enough.

So where did all this insane activity come from? Whose idea was it, anyway? And since it makes everyone neurotic and dangerous and ruins the planet, why can't we stop doing it?

Well, because it works. It works to keep people fragmented, to keep them from thinking about real things. It enables a caste of individuals who are genetically incapable of integrated thinking to define the world in terms of a board game, so that they can believe they are winning—which is the closest they can come to a functional definition of living.

And because they control the resources, it keeps the rest of us hopping.

Because being lazy is being present. And that's dangerous as hell.

Substance Over Symbol

———◦———

" ... it does not pay to cherish symbols
  when substance
  lies so close at hand..."

—Audre Lorde

These lines are from Lorde's poem "Walking Our Boundaries." I have selected them, because they are such a powerful reminder.

As a Lesbian-feminist, I have a free mind, I have an overwhelming vision that can provide solace for any grief, I have a passion, I have a purpose: I have substance.

And yet, I am frequently mesmerized by mainstream culture's obsession with money, with "job security," with predictions and prognoses. Manipulating symbols, I lose the substance of living, and I lose the ever-present moment that is the only possibility for possibilities.

African American Lesbian poet Audre Lorde reminds us again and again in her writing to look for that lost chord. And we *can* find it, because Lesbians embody the substance for which the rest of the world must have symbols.

Chemistry

"There's nothing colder than chemistry."

—Anita Loos

Strange words from the author of *Gentlemen Prefer Blondes*.

Anita Loos, one of Hollywood's most successful screenwriters, was a woman of contradictions. She was very small in stature and went out of her way all her life to dress in a style that can only be characterized as little-girlish. She was attracted to older (and taller) male father figures, and went so far as to marry one of them, who promptly reversed the poles of the relationship by becoming utterly helpless and dependent on her—but who somehow still retained a contemptuous and patronizing attitude toward her, claiming that she was responsible for his ruin even as she continued to support him!

Perhaps her attraction to these older men stemmed from her unusual relationship to her father, which was very suggestive of emotional, if not physical, incest. In any event, Anita felt a need to mask her sophistication and brilliant wit behind a childlike facade. Perhaps this voluntary self-neutralizing provided a protective coloring that was necessary for an ambitious and competitive woman to survive in Hollywood. How else could she keep from threatening her male colleagues in an environment based on the objectification of women? How else, as an attractive woman, could she meet the constant sexual harassment without attracting the reputation of being "frigid" or "easy?"

But, let's get back to her quotation. Chemistry—the excitement generated by the recognition of mutual addictions? Did Anita feel a chemical attraction to father figures, looking for a "fix" for an addiction cultivated in early childhood by her betraying, but seemingly loving father? Did her husband feel a similar chemical attraction to this obviously competent woman, based on his own addictive need to find a good mommy? And how quickly this kind of chemistry plays itself out in a game of escalating exploitation! It boils down to cold transactions: "I'll be the mommy financially and domestically, if you'll be the daddy out in public and protect me from the other predatory males." And from here, the dynamic can easily slide into blackmail and extortion, a barter system full of sharp penalties and ever-present threats.

Gentlemen Prefer Blondes, seemingly a glorification of "chemistry," is actually a very graphic depiction of the exchange system behind traditional heterosexual courtship: economic protection in exchange for sexual access. In her book, all parties are comfortable with exploiting the system. What Anita did not expose was the underlying condition of disenfranchisement that has driven women into the sexual barter system—in other words, the enslavement of women. Needless to say, that analysis would never have topped the best-seller list.

Chemistry is a poor index of attraction. A better index would be mutual interests, common friends, compatible values, or shared spiritual goals.

Impossible Dreams

"My Cheechum used to tell me that when the government gives you something, they take all that you have in return — your pride, your dignity, all the things that make you a living soul. When they are sure they have everything they give you a blanket to cover your shame. She said that the churches with their talk about God, the Devil, heaven and hell, and the schools that taught children to be ashamed, were all part of that government... She used to say that all our people wore blankets, each in his own way... I no longer need my blanket to survive... The blanket only destroys, it doesn't give warmth."

—Maria Campbell

These are the words of Maria Campbell, a Canadian Metis born in 1940 in northern Saskatchewan. In her book, *Halfbreed*, she tells of her struggle against an artificially imposed status.

Under Canadian law, First Nation peoples were rigidly and arbitrarily divided into categories that were recognized or not recognized by law. First Nation peoples were designated "registered treaty Indians" or "registered non-treaty Indians," based on past relations with the government. Then there were the "non-registered Indians," a group that included First Nation women who married non-First Nation men. First Nation men, however, did not lose their registered status for marrying outsiders. After 1940, the Metis, those First Nation people with mixed ancestry, were denied any recognition as a legally defined group.

Maria's great-grandmother and spiritual mentor, Cheechum, understood these classifications to be a strategy of war: "The white man saw that that was a more powerful weapon than anything else with which to beat the Halfbreeds, and he used it and still does today... They try to make you hate your people."

Maria's struggle for recognition, for escape from poverty, for education was as a painful one in which her dreams had a way of turning into nightmares. The relocation that was supposed to create a happy family was no more than an exchange of rural poverty for urban poverty. The prostitution that was supposed to result in a glamourous lifestyle resulted in no material improvement, but the sense that "something inside" had died.

Finally, as an activist, Maria found the courage to let go of the impossible dreams that a capitalist and colonial society dangle in front of the oppressed, and to work for the realizable dreams of social change: "I've stopped being the idealistic shiny eyed young woman I once was... I believe that one day, very soon, people will set aside their differences and come together as one. Maybe not because we love one another, but because we will need one another to survive. Then together we will fight our common enemies. Change will come because this time we won't give up."

Integrity

"The outsiders... would bind themselves not to continue to make money in any profession, but to cease all competition and to practice their profession experimentally, in the interests of research and for the love of the work itself, when they had earned enough to live upon."

—Virginia Woolf

Virginia must have been distressed to watch her lover, Vita Sackville-West, squander her talents in writing Danielle-Steele-type romances for the popular market. It must have also galled her to see her lover's books climb to the top of the best-seller lists and go into second and third printings, while her own radical and meticulously-crafted novels could only garner small, elite audiences during her lifetime. And how did it feel to read her lover's hetero-patriarchal romances where the author's alter-ego is clearly the male character?

Today, Vita's books are not widely read. There are few, if any, university courses devoted to her work. In fact, Vita is probably best known for her gardening and for *Portrait of A Marriage*, a book containing her secret journal of her Lesbian passion for Violet Trefusis, a journal that was found in a locked gladstone bag after her death.

On the other hand, Virginia Woolf's work continues to grow in popularity and in literary acclaim. Her sales have far outstripped Vita's, and her books have entered the traditional canon of English literature, having been recognized for decades as foundations of anglo-european Women's Studies.

Virginia lived by her own lights, and she never wrote commercially, because she never needed to financially.

Virginia Woolf was born into privilege and had an annuity sufficient to keep her in a middle-class lifestyle, with her own home and servants. She could afford to tell the truth. In some ways her life was easy.

On the other hand, it couldn't have been easy to see her work so overlooked, so misunderstood, so lionized for wrong reasons in her lifetime. As a survivor of incest, she desperately needed to be validated. She might have known that her books, so honest and so far ahead of their time, would only bring about the replication of the lack of credibility she experienced in her childhood.

At the end of *To the Lighthouse*, the heroine Lilly Briscoe is attempting to paint a landscape. The formidable patriarch of the family is agitated, standing at her shoulder, silently commanding her attention. She refuses to give it to him, stays focused on her work, and administers the final brush stroke. Whatever the merits of the painting, she has achieved an epic victory in that "she has had her vision."

Virginia Woolf, in choosing "to cease all competition and to practice [her] profession experimentally," also had her vision, and the patriarchal stranglehold on English literature has never been the same.

Karma

—————————

"You create your own destiny when you are true to yourself, when you strive to reach your dreams, yes. But if a woman is raped... was that her karma? No way! That was not her fault; she didn't create patriarchy or woman hating."

—Z Budapest

Patriarchy has always found ways to blame women for the horrors it perpetrates against us. In the past, the rape victim was accused of promiscuity if she wasn't a virgin and wishful thinking or seduction if she was. If she smiled at her assailant, she asked for it. If she didn't smile, she provoked him. If she was wearing a skirt, it was too short. If she was wearing pants, they were too tight. Wherever she was whenever it happened, she should have known better. How dare she go out at night? How dare she go anywhere alone? How dare she use a parking deck? How dare she be on campus after dark? How dare she forget to lock a window, double dead-bolt the door? Judges have even gone so far as to find little girls guilty of corrupting the morals of their fathers!

Now that women have begun to break the silence about our experiences and we are realizing that one out of three girls will be raped before she is eighteen, patriarchy has had to become a little more subtle about finding ways to blame the victim.

What has it done? It has tried to appeal to women's rising desire to become empowered. New Age philosophy would teach us that the way to this empowerment is to realize that we are responsible for "creating our own reality." It would have us believe that we have chosen the things that happen to us—that our rapists are people we have "attracted" into our experience to teach us karmic lessons we need to learn!

I have heard victimized women tell me they chose their abusive families before they were born, that they must have been a rapist in a former life; otherwise they wouldn't have needed to be raped in this one!

It's understandable why some women embrace this New Age philosophy. It enables them to feel some control in a world where random violence against girls and women is universal and institutionalized.

But this sense of control is an illusion. There is no real power in believing we have chosen—or need—our abuse. In fact, it becomes a rationale for passivity. Why intervene in the torture of a three-year old, if you believe she is really an ancient soul getting a karmic lesson from a chosen teacher?

Woman-hating is the fashion in patriarchy, and like any fashion, it changes style with predictable frequency to reflect the popular trends. It strives to appear new, indispensable, on the cutting edge. But there is no radical chic in blaming women for what men do.

The really new look for women is the look we get when we begin to hold men accountable for their actions.

Thirst-Enduring

⟶⟶●◆●⟵

"We have a word that means thirst-enduring."
— Marie Chona

Marie Chona, a Papago Indian woman born in the 19th century, was describing her language to the woman who was taking down her oral history.

Thirst-enduring. A word that shapes perception. Where "thirsty" implies a passive state of deprivation, "thirst-enduring" connotes an active and creative response. "Thirst-enduring" sets the mind to strategizing, instead of reinforcing a scenario of desperation.

In a competitive and consumer culture, our vocabulary breaks down into the "haves" and "have-nots," with little attention to (or vocabulary for) the strategies employed by the so-called "have-nots." This deficiency of language would rob oppressed people of a sense of our own agency. It would lead us to believe our only option is to cross over into the ranks of the "haves" as quickly as possible and at any price.

Women are thirst-enduring. We owe it to ourselves to expand our vocabularies to celebrate our unending resourcefulness, our spiritual plenitude, and our stunning ability to demonstrate generosity and abundance in the middle of the deepest drought.

Miracles

"Where there is great love there are always miracles."
—Willa Cather

Belief in miracles hardly seems a radical idea. Isn't that the theory, like the home in heaven, that keeps so many women from taking responsibility for creating change in the here and now?

But what about spiritual power? Look at role models and mentors. What is the process by which a woman at Point A gets herself to Point B? Doesn't she have an idea in mind first, some mental concept of what Point B looks like—or at least an inkling of how the woman behaves who is not settling for Point A? Maybe she caught a glimpse of these in a book, or in the example of some female relative—a spinster aunt or other family eccentric, or maybe from watching some of the women around her, or maybe she came up with it all by herself in some primitive recess of her own mind that intuitively comprehends a way of living beyond what is going on around her. What exactly is that capacity to see beyond our present circumstances and our current limitations? And if that capacity is the cradle of radical change, do we have the ability to expand that function of our psyches?

I believe that we do. We can expand it by exercising our imagination in radical ways. The function of the dominant culture is to appropriate the imaginative facilities of women to serve patriarchal interests. It does this by presenting us with subtle and not-so-subtle images designed to generate fear and dread. As a result, women monitor and police ourselves for subversive behavior or potentially disruptive ideas.

We can take back our fantasy life. We can use our imagination consciously to invent the lives we want. We can flood our consciousness with empowering images, rituals, fables, and stories about ourselves and about other women. We can consciously celebrate our strengths and our victories.

To do this may require the recruitment of another area of our consciousness: our faith—that is, our capacity to believe that there's any point in imagining. Reprogramming requires the faith that we can and do have access to power, no matter what the material (dominant cultural) picture would tell us. Faith can be blind belief that deceives women into making disastrous choices. An example of this is the belief that God will stand by a woman who stands by her man. But real faith is faith in oneself, one's uncolonized self.

Faith and imagination work together. And, when both are free from the pollution of male dominant creeds and scenarios, they are miracle workers. And they do work in mysterious ways, but not by petitioning—which is the *modus operandi* of patriarchal religion. When women cultivate the discipline to maintain the faith that keeps our imaginative functions working for empowerment—and it is a discipline—the miracles come. And when we do, we are also synergistic and symbiotic, and resultant miracle can be greater than the sum of both.

Writer, editor, and journalist Willa Cather did love. She loved women. And she loved herself enough not to settle for the life that was expected of her. And that was a miracle.

The Greatest Secret

"... I could have become a perpetrator. How many other survivors could say the same? But we are not permitted to speak of this, except perhaps, if we are lucky, in the sanctum of individual counseling... Knowing this about myself has made going back, forgetting what I can't quite remember, an impossibility."
—Lynne Yamaguchi Fletcher

Lynne is writing this in the context of explaining a poem she wrote from the perspective of a child molester. She is telling one of the greatest secrets a radical feminist can share. It is also a secret for which we must learn to find vocabulary and process.

How many times have we seen radical women's organizations run along the lines of a dysfunctional family? How many amazon activists have we seen go down with illness and disability, because they neglected to eat, to sleep, to take time out, to play? And how many times have powerful leaders been willing to overlook contradictions and inconsistencies in their personal lives and their political ideologies—especially when racism, ageism, ableism, and classism were involved? Margaret Sanger, the intrepid pioneer for birth control, advocated sterilization of the poor and the unemployed, and was guilty of negligence toward her daughter, a negligence that may have contributed to the child's death! Elizabeth Cady Stanton, a leader of the women's suffrage movement, demonstrated a shocking degree of racism and classism when she called for literacy tests and educational qualifications as voting requirements.

More and more women are speaking out against the "isms" in women's organizations, but how about the "isms" in our personal lives? Why so much silence? Because the accusation of "abusive behaviors" is frequently a call to arms or the signal for an all-out witch-hunt, and in the live-and-let-live philosophy of recovery, we are more likely to detach from the woman with these behaviors. And, it's true, if enough friends detach, a woman may be led to examine her actions. Most likely, however, she will just accuse everyone of betraying her and look for new friends among women more damaged by their conditioning.

Lynne's quotation goes to the heart of the problem. When we are exposed to violations as a child—be they ideological or behavioral—we do internalize the perspective of the perpetrator. It is no more shameful to discover we are carrying these mental and emotional viruses, than it is to realize we were infected with a disease by a rapist. The victim should not have to deny, repress, hide, or justify these toxic attitudes. Instead, she should be able to recruit support from her allies in identifying them and replacing them with healthy and *chosen* behaviors. And we should not feel terrified at the prospect of confronting them. In fact, as radical feminists, it is helpful for us to point them out.

When we all have the kind of openness expressed in Lynne's quotation, we will see a new day for our movement—and the removal of a formidable obstacle to our empowerment!

Being an Outsider

"This was the summer when for a long time she had not been a member. She belonged to no club and was a member of nothing in the world. Frankie had become an unjoined person who hung around in the doorways, and she was afraid."

—Carson McCullers

This is a quotation describing the central character from *Member of the Wedding*, Frankie. She is a girl suspended between the childhood "freedom" of disenfranchisement and the "empowerment" that comes with socialization to adult roles. She still spends time with the much younger child from next door. She still spends time in the kitchen with Berenice, the African American woman employed by the family. The girls her age are shunning her. She has resisted the hetero-patriarchal conditioning they embrace. She still lives outside the formal boundaries of grown-up racism. But she is not Berenice's daughter, and she's not a child anymore. She does not feel she belongs to any class or to any category. Yet.

Frankie becomes "initiated" in a scene that is a cross between date rape and child molesting. When she tries to attach herself to her brother and his new bride, she experiences her final ejection from childhood. At the end of the book, Frankie has begun the process of socializing herself into white, heterosexual, racist classist society.

It takes fortitude to be an outsider. It's difficult not to focus negatively on the "insiders." It's also difficult to pass up the few tidbits of privilege that may come our way, to pass up the temptation to scapegoat—even if just for a few minutes—another woman who may temporarily be even more of an outsider in some transitory subset of outsiderhood.

Being a perpetual outsider makes you feel crazy, makes you doubt yourself, makes you consider killing yourself. Being a perpetual outsider also gives you an unparalleled perspective on what is really going on. Most great artists were hopeless outsiders. Creating a private world of meaning through their art was their only escape.

Outsiders can experience difficulty bonding with other outsiders, because two outsiders have the potential of forming a small "inside," which can challenge every strategy we have so assiduously cultivated to endure our outsiderhood.

If you are one of the outsiders, work to be an insider to yourself. That is the key to survival. And if you cultivate a powerful enough spiritual discipline, you will find that sooner or later, there will be women who are asking to belong to your club.

Temptation to Compromise

<hr>

" ... [the challenge] lost the truth. It lost the real and basic feelings of the grassroots. Because all the guys was in again—the big wheels and the ones from Mississippi and all these guys that you see [who] now jumped up on the back of this and became big famous people."

—Fannie Lou Hamer

Fannie Lou Hamer was speaking about the 1968 Democratic convention, when a coalition of Democrats calling themselves "Loyalists" challenged the seating of party regulars on the grounds that these regulars had continued to discriminate against Black candidates—in violation of the mandate of the National Democratic Party. The convention did vote to unseat the regulars, and Fannie Lou and the other "Loyalists" were seated instead. This was considered a victory for the civil rights movement, because the challengers in 1964 had *not* been seated.

But Fannie Lou had mixed feelings about the 1968 convention. In 1964, she had attended with members of the radical Mississippi Freedom Democratic Party to challenge the seating, but four years later the challengers represented a coalition with moderates, including several white liberals. Fannie Lou was concerned that the political structure of Mississippi would be changed without changing the relationship of the poor to that structure. The MFDP had wanted outright grants of free land, long-term low-interest loans for farm cooperatives, guaranteed annual income, fair representation for Blacks and poor people in all state agencies, expanded day care, free medical care, and free higher education.

Fannie Lou had worked long and hard on behalf of the rural poor, and she had led the fight when it was most dangerous. Now that the Civil Rights Movement had begun to win popular support (at least outside Mississippi), and was beginning to attract liberal whites, a whole new class of men were jumping on the band-wagon—and Fannie Lou was dead right about the result.

The radical fight is lonely and hard, and it's tempting to leap at the chance for coalition with our "allies." But it is always wise to question the price of this help. What would the United States look like today, if the civil rights movement had stayed true to its radical roots? What if the women's suffrage workers had stayed committed to the fight for the reforms that they were so convinced the vote would bring? Today, Lesbians are being offered coalition from a number of other groups—on the basis of our "sexual preference." What does that narrow defini-tion of Lesbianism do to our radical feminist agenda?

Fannie Lou lived to see a rising class of middle-class Black male professionals take over the positions and run for the offices created by the courage and persistence of the poorest of the poor, whose interests were always the first to be sac-rificed in the name of political expediency "for all Blacks."

The formation of class structures within an oppressed class is no cause for celebration—but generally marks a downturn in the ability of that group to organize effec-tively. Can we, as Lesbians, learn from the history of other liberation movements—and can we resist the temp-tation to compromise?

Reason and Logic

"I'll not listen to reason... Reason always means what someone else has got to say."

—Elizabeth Gaskell

As a nineteenth-century woman author, Elizabeth Gaskell had good reason to distrust "reason."

Reason is deceptive, because it masquerades as the voice of ultimate authority when, in fact, it is the exclusive property of the class who owns the right to name.

The woman who cannot name her emotional abuse can be characterized as "unreasonable" for wanting to leave a husband—especially if he's sober and "a good provider." A woman who is unable to express the source of her dissatisfaction can also seem "unreasonable" when she leaves a well-paying job.

Because we are not yet fluent in naming our experiences, our deepest and soundest impulses often fall under the category of "unreasonable" in patriarchy.

"Trust your gut," is, at this point in our evolution, the most reasonable advice women can follow.

Women's Studies

"Women's studies... actively and aggressively supports women in becoming and remaining heterosexual; it actively seeks to encourage women to believe that the personal, political, economic, and health problems associated with heterosexuality for women should be struggled with rather than avoided—that these problems are inevitable but more or less solvable... rather than that they are unsolvable but definitely evitable."

—Marilyn Frye

This quotation by Lesbian philosopher Marilyn Frye is about crazy-making. The Lesbian feminist who looks to the Women's Studies department for some sanity and grounding in the patriarchal halls of academia can be in for a terrible surprise. She may find that, although there is a token acknowledgment of her existence, the reduction of Lesbianism to a diversity issue is a more deadly form of invisibility than the more blatant erasure of her presence in the men's studies curricula that comprises the rest of the university.

And not just Women's Studies. As Lesbianism becomes more and more "tolerated" or "accepted" by the mainstream, the more we are expected to reciprocate with gratitude, it being considered bad manners to harbor a prejudice against heterosexualism when the straights have worked so hard to overcome their fear and disgust of us.

Everyone likes to search for lost objects in places that are familiar and well-lit. But the simple fact remains: The lost object can only be found where it was actually lost, not where we think we lost it, or where we hope we lost it, or where we'd like to say we found it.

As Marilyn's quotation points out, without a critique of heterosexuality, the key to many women's miseries will not be found. Women's Studies encourages women to divert our precious resources in a search that cannot prove fruitful, because the key to women's lost freedoms does not lie in the house of patriarchy. It lies in the terrifying regions of taboo childhood memories and the community of women who have renounced the privileges of patriarchy to explore our native culture.

Perspective

—⟫●⟪—

"Who can laugh at my Marsh Rosemary, or who can cry, for that matter? The gray primness of the plant is made up from a hundred colors if you look close enough to find them. This Marsh Rosemary stands in her own place, and holds her dry leaves and tiny blossoms steadily toward the same sun that the pink lotus blooms for, or the white rose."

—Sarah Orne Jewett

This is a passage by Sarah Orne Jewett quoted in an essay by Willa Cather. The essay is called "Miss Jewett," and Willa is using the quotation to illustrate the modesty that Sarah always exhibited toward her own "sketches"—the word she used to describe her short stories. Willa's ostensibly favorable essay is blatantly patronizing toward her former mentor and may possibly be a pay-back for Jewett's accusation that Cather's male lover in one of her stories was "something of a masquerade."

Willa Cather, a Lesbian novelist, wrote rugged books about emigrant pioneers, priests in the wilderness, and boys at the front. Her protagonists, often represented in the first person, were frequently male, and the strongest relationships in her books were between men.

Sarah Orne Jewett was also a Lesbian, but her work focuses on relationships between women—especially between "spinsters." Her work reflects a matriarchal context, and most of the stories are set in rural communities. I would argue that Willa's perception that Sarah's subject matter was limited is only evidence of Willa's internalizing of the patriarchal value system.

As Jewett points out in her quotation, the Marsh Rosemary, in fact, holds hundreds of colors. Its "gray primness" is only a question of perspective. For one who is close enough to observe the incredible spectrum of color represented in the flower, the homogeneity of the "pink lotus" or the "white rose" must seem to be emblematic of a more limited and less spectacular species.

And so, indeed, as a Lesbian-feminist, I find the works of Willa Cather. Her book about World War I, valorizing patriotism and a soldier's life, was dated even in its own time, as men returning from the front began to create their own literature about the horror and waste of war.

Willa painted on a wide and panoramic canvas, using "epic" and "universal" themes that are so near and dear to the hearts of men: colonization of the wild, man-made religious moral dilemmas, love of one's country. Jewett's work, on the other hand, was integrated with the Lesbianism she lived, and because of that, it has a holographic quality, where all of the whole is contained in even a tiny fragment. Willa's work, however "universal" it might appear, is split at the root from her experience of herself as a woman, and—in this reader's eyes—does not hold up today.

Frequently a woman who is integrating her own experience on deep psychic levels—almost impossible in patriarchy!—chooses to retreat to an insular world for a time, or even for years. To assume that, because of this, she will have insufficient experience to produce great art is to refute the work of Virginia Woolf, Emily Dickinson, and Sarah Orne Jewett. As with the Marsh Rosemary, the fault lies in the focal distance of the viewer.

Controversy

"Innovators are inevitably controversial."

—Eva Le Gallienne

Eva Le Gallienne knew whereof she spoke. Still in her twenties, she turned down a promising career as one of Broadway's hottest ingenues in order to found her own theatre company, the Civic Repertory. She had a vision of performing the classics in repertory and offering them to the public at prices affordable to the working classes. Part of her vision included performing works that offered more serious roles for women than the standard Broadway fluff. And she hired women administrators.

Needless to say, Eva was a Lesbian.

Eva's actions threatened the New York theatre establishment, and, unlike Kit Cornell or Lynne Fontanne, she did not hide behind the facade of a "respectable" marriage. She paid dearly for her integrity, when the critics, thinly masking their homophobia, would score her performances over and over again with references to her "lack of passion" or her "intellectualism."

She became lovers with one of the actors at the Civic, and when Josephine Hutchinson filed for a divorce from her husband, the New York papers had a field day. Eva, who had never gone to any lengths to disguise her Lesbianism, was nevertheless devastated by the publicity.

The innovator is controversial. She may not be prepared for controversy, she may not have the temperament to meet the challenges, and she may not have realized how many of those around her—family and friends—would be affected by her notoriety.

The innovator often travels to a different drum; that's why she's able to approach things in a way no one has ever thought of before. But that is also why she is often painfully naive about human nature and the ways of the world. Getting support or asking for help may not have been things she ever thought of or learned how to do. She may have believed that the world, in awe of her creativity or originality, would beat a path to her door. She may have believed that excellence, brilliance, or being in the right would provide sufficient insurance against persecution.

Remember Joan of Arc? She crowned the king, led the army to victory after victory, and had the saints communicating with her directly. What happened to her? The army deserted her, the king betrayed her, and her own church burned her alive.

The lesson here is to expect the controversy and learn where your support lies before you need to call on it.

Fear

" ... considering how dangerous everything is nothing is
really very frightening."

—Gertrude Stein

Gertrude Stein was a problem for the Nazis. Everybody
knew she lived in Paris, and everybody knew she was
Jewish. And everybody who was anybody loved
Gertrude Stein. The Nazis knew that if they deported
Gertrude Stein to a concentration camp, there would be
an international outcry. Now, why there wasn't this kind
of outcry over the deportation of the Jews who were not
Gertrude Stein is a question that has been asked many
times in the decades since the war, and one that has never
received a satisfactory answer.

In any event, the Nazis were reluctant to deport
Gertrude. So they struck a deal. They sent word to her
that she was about to be deported, but that, if she acted
swiftly, she would be allowed to cross over into
Switzerland unharmed.

Obviously they were not familiar with Gertrude's work,
or they would have realized that she had risen above
grammar and syntax. Certainly after an achievement like
that, she wasn't going to let any mere government offi-
cials dictate to her. She said that France was her home,
and that if the other Jews were not allowed to leave, she
certainly wasn't going to either.

She and Alice, who was also Jewish, did leave Paris, however. They moved to a village in the south of France for
the duration of the war. Gertrude went by another name,

but everybody knew who she was anyway. "A rose is a rose is a rose."

Was Gertrude afraid? I think it trivializes her choice to portray her as a dotty, eccentric woman who was oblivious to the dangers of her situation. I believe that she was very concerned for her life. But I also believe she understood that her safety lay in her gut understanding of home, and for her, that home was France. As the *I Ching* says, "There are worse things to lose than one's life."

As a Lesbian and a survivor of an unhappy childhood, Gertrude Stein had fled America to live in France. After years of being overshadowed by her arrogant brother and repudiated by the world of "belles lettres," she had finally come into her voice and her identity in her adopted country. Perhaps she knew that exile back to her birth home would be as dangerous to her as deportation. For Gertrude—who she was, was what she wrote, was where she lived, was how she lived, was with whom she lived. She refused to be fragmented, even by threat of death. As always, she reserved for herself the right to define her terms.

And Gertrude survived the Nazis. And her writing survived the critics. And the record of her life with Alice continues to survive the homophobes.

Women in Combat

"So you see now, don't you, why I smile when you ask about the problems for women combatants. Are we big enough? Fast enough? Can we carry a one-hundred-pound pack? Will we cause fighting among the men? These are questions for children, and there are no children up here."

—Lorena

Lorena is one of the Guatemalan "compañeras," or freedom fighters of the Guatemalan National Revolutionary Union whose story is documented in Jennifer Harbury's book *Bridge of Courage*.

Lorena writes that the most difficult part of her adjustment to becoming a guerrilla fighter was not the physical hardship, or even the combat itself, but her struggle with "what a woman should or shouldn't be, should or shouldn't do, should or shouldn't think."

Falling in love with a fellow revolutionary, Lorena had to confront her terrors about being in a sexual relationship outside of marriage. Her cultural conditioning had taught her that this would render her unworthy of respect. She had to do battle with the terrorists in her own psyche in order to win control of her sexuality.

Later, finding herself pregnant, she was forced to choose between leaving the mountains and her partner, or having an abortion. She chose the abortion, and the experience was traumatic and shameful for her.

When she returned to the mountains, she found herself angry and resentful toward her comrade-at-arms, whose biology and cultural conditioning prevented him from sharing the consequences of their "equal" relationship.

Before Lorena had a chance to work through her feelings about her partner, he was fatally wounded in combat. Rushing to the scene of battle to be with him when he died, Lorena was confronted with a spectacle of grisly mutilation. The enemy had gotten there first.

For a year, she struggled with nightmares and madness, but with the support of the compañeros and compañeras, she eventually recovered, and at the time of her telling the story, she had been fighting for ten years.

Today debate rages on about women in combat positions, Lesbians in the military, women at male military institutions, but, in Lorena's words, "The real question for all of us, men and women alike, is whether or not we have the emotional flexibility and strength to survive the realities of this terrible war."

False Equations

>=•=<

"Why are women... so much more interesting to men than men are to women?"

—Virginia Woolf

This question has great relevance to the woman artist.

I had a friend in art school. In her drawing classes, she was required to sketch female and male live models.

Like the majority of women, she had been a victim of sexual assault as a child. She found herself numbing out, splitting off, and becoming physically ill on the days when she was required to focus for two hours on a naked man, genitals exposed, and interpret what she was seeing on paper.

When she shared her feelings with other women in the class (a radical act in itself!), many of them admitted to similar dissociative experiences with the male models. My friend went to her professor with "her" problem. He was snide and patronizing. He allowed her to skip the days when men were modeling, but he lowered her grade substantially. After all, the men in the class have to draw the naked women, don't they? He was only being fair.

Why is it that women who claim heterosexuality as their "sexual preference" don't paint, sculpt, photograph naked men in anywhere near the numbers that men render nude women? Why is it that our greatest women poets do not write ode after ode about the glory of the male body? And certainly our women musicians are not dreaming of Johnny with the light brown hair.

Maybe women just aren't that interested in their lovers' bodies? Lesbian art gives the lie to that. The female body is a popular, if not dominant, theme in Lesbian visual art. And in Lesbian poetry. And in Lesbian literature. "Womyn's music" is nothing if not a celebration of Amazon passion.

So what would account for this discrepancy? What if the answer lies in the fact that women are the initial objects of desire and identification for both genders when we are infants. What if the first lesson for all of us is to associate the breast with pleasure, nurturance, and fulfillment? What if Lesbianism is the natural state of all women, and what if it is only the unnatural imposition of brutal sanctions and pervasive brainwashing that creates an artificial state of identity with the colonizers, a state known as heterosexuality?

What if women naturally preferred women, and—more to the point—what if we were all free to act on that preference?

Advice

"I went home, followed these directions rigidly for
months, and came perilously near to losing my
mind."

—Charlotte Perkins Gilman

Charlotte Perkins Gilman was a nineteenth-century
American writer and social critic. She is referring to her
doctor's advice on how to treat a depression brought on
by her reaction to married life and motherhood. Her doctor was a Philadelphia neurologist, a specialist in
women's nervous diseases. This was his advice: "Live as
domestic a life as possible. Have your child with you all
the time... Lie down an hour after each meal. Have but
two hours intellectual life a day. And never touch pen,
brush or pencil as long as you live."

Appalling advice. Not unlike the advice given to Virginia
Woolf for her emotional problems. She was also sent to
bed and advised not to write.

Charlotte's doctor had gained his reputation, because his
"Rest Cure" did do the trick: Women who had been following his regime for months suddenly welcomed the
chance to return to the routine of domestic duties that
had previously brought on the depression. The breaking
of a woman's spirit was considered a successful cure. In
other words, solitary confinement makes prison routine
look good.

Does this all seem like ancient history? Today there is a
new fad for treating depression. Anti-depressants. Today
women's depression is attributed to biochemical imbal-

ances in the brain that supposedly require chemical treatment. And do the anti-depressants work? It depends on how you define "cure."

If the point of a woman's life is to continue to function in a round of daily chores—then yes, they are a miracle cure. If the point of a woman's life is to achieve autonomy through remembering the repressed, integrating the fragments, breaking through the brainwashing, and defining the meaning of life on her own terms—then maybe they are not so miraculous.

It is my belief that the greater a woman's capacity for ecstatic experience and wildness, the greater her depression with what passes for normal living. Her depression, her apathy, her discomfort are her greatest guides. "Normal" will not bring her out of depression. The bar is set higher for her than for many others, and she will need to make a grand leap of faith to clear it. She is called to live a larger life, to be a spiritual seeker—an artist or activist perhaps, or maybe just a thorough eccentric! What if anti-depressants just lower the bar so that she can clear her obstacles with effort far under her potential? And if she is a true athlete of life, where is the sport in that?

Charlotte wrote a famous story about her so-called treatment: "The Yellow Wallpaper." Unlike the tragic protagonist of the story, Charlotte rebelled against her treatment, took charge of her life, and went on to become a self-determined and self-fulfilled lecturer and writer and women's rights activist.

Plain-Speaking

———⟫•⟨———

"It is monstrous to betray your child, bitch."
                                    —Andrea Dworkin

Thus spoke Andrea Dworkin in *Mercy*, one of the greatest women's novels ever written, being a stream-of-consciousness depiction of the mind of a raped and mindfucked woman.

Another favorite quotation of mine by Andrea is: "The perpetrator is the problem, stupid." This quotation was in an article about Nicole Simpson, the wife of the famous athlete, who was battered, stalked, and terrorized by him, and finally murdered. Media focus had been scrutinizing the lifestyle and choices of Nicole.

Too often, as women living under patriarchy, we can fall into analyzing what we as women could have done, should have done, might do better next time. As Andrea pointed out, the *perpetrator* is the problem.

And her quotation about mothers is also to the point. We can agonize over the impossible conditions for single mothers, the lack of day care, lack of safe housing, and so forth. But the bottom line is as simple as that: "It is monstrous to betray your child, bitch."

Why does that statement arouse such anxiety, such a storm of protest? The language directed at innocent children is ten times worse, and a million times more prevalent.

I believe that Andrea's statement scares us precisely because it is the pure voice of the child advocate—the one we have become complicitous in silencing. It is the one that will indict us along with our mothers, the one with the memories, the one with the dreams, the one with the passionate sense of justice, and the one with the murderous rage. The voice of the child advocate will disrupt every aspect of our adult lives. It will not be assimilated. It must be silenced or heeded.

As a good Lesbian-feminist, I want to give every woman her due. I want to look at every situation through an analysis of all the oppressions. But, sometimes, when I am feeling confused, I ask myself—quick!—no thinking allowed: "What do you really think?" And the answer from the gut is often as simple as "I don't trust her," "Fuck, no," or just plain "Bitch."

Plain-speaking among women is a radical virtue. It often has to by-pass the complicated circuitry in our consciousness that we had to construct in order to protect the areas of denial. Thank the goddess for women like Andrea, who have spent a season in hell, battled their way out of terror and confusion, and then conscientiously and courageously descended again to bring us back the precious, plain-speaking language for these horrendous experiences.

Harsh Realities

"Men don't take us seriously because they're not physically afraid of us."
—slogan on Always Causing Legal Unrest button

We need to learn to scare men. That means not only being prepared to defend ourselves physically, but also legally, academically, socially, artistically and spiritually. We need to show them that we are not afraid to fight, not afraid to hurt or destroy them, not afraid to sue the pants off them, not afraid to get custody, to get child support, to get damages. We need to show that we can organize women workers, women teachers, women union members, women managers, women students, mothers, witches, survivors of sexual abuse, women health care workers—that we can picket, we can occupy, we can exploit the media, we can embarrass, we can upstage, we can use their own words and their own systems against them.

Being assertive is fine. But women were assertive for years about sexual harassment, and all we got for our troubles was a chuck on the chin or the pink slip. But—voilá! Just a few lawsuits, just a few six-figure settlements—and now, suddenly the workplace, the military, the universities are flooded with videos, posters, workshops, and policies about the issue.

Women who balk at learning to be dangerous are *not* wimps. We have a long history of victimization, and I believe that we still carry in our race memory the trauma of the Burning Times, when millions of women—the brightest and best, were burned all over Europe.

193

Traditionally, the woman who fought back could expect to be incarcerated for mental illness, or murdered by her husband who could expect a sympathetic jury. Few of our mothers carried weapons. Few of our teachers encouraged us to learn fighting skills. And few of our peers are dangerous yet.

But we can start by examining our discomfort. We can take the information that we have learned to forget or split off, and begin to collate. How many times have we been sexually assaulted, exhibited to, pressured to have sex against our will, sexually harassed, ridiculed, trivialized or excluded as women? What do we remember about discrimination? Allow these incidents and episodes to synapse with one another. Watch the pattern that emerges, the matrix in which you have lived your life—running it like an obstacle course. Yes, it is a system. It is a conspiracy, a war.

They hate us that much. That is terrifying. We can wear all the lipstick in the world and smile the biggest "yessir" in the world. We can hobble ourselves, and bare twice as much skin as them in the workplace. We can bedeck ourselves with capitulating frills and bows, we can decorate ourselves. We can ritualize and fetishize our hair, our nails, our faces.

And then we can defer to them. We can sleep with them. We can flatter them. We can do their work for them and let them take the credit. We can forgive them, excuse them, cover for them. We can make of point of never asking for anything, never complaining, never talking about them to other women.

We can do all this, and still they will hate us. Isn't it time we tried scaring them?

Fashion

❦

"I see shoes not made to walk in, clothes not made to work in,
   women not meant to last."

—D.A. Clarke

These are lines from Lesbian-feminist D.A.Clarke's poem "and everywhere unicorns."

Planned obsolescence is another definition of fashion. The nails will chip or grow out. The perm will go flat or grow out. So will the dye. The hemlines will go up or down. The shoes will get scuffed or torn, the straps will wear through, the heels will break off or wear down. The stockings will run. The mascara will run. The lipstick will get eaten off.

But what about the woman who is trying to keep one step ahead of all this destruction? Where is she behind the makeup, under the $100 hair? Does she have any sense of her permanence?

And what about the Lesbian, who has liberated herself from the self-conscious rituals of hetero-patriarchy? Do we have any sense of permanence?

With what has our community replaced these rituals? Do we pounce on one another's vestigial tailings of racism, ageism, fat phobia with the same glee that a heterosexual woman might note the new grey hair of a rival, or the run in her stocking? Do we confront one another as allies in a struggle against a common internalized oppressor, or do we use our discovery of incorrect behavior as a way of dismissing or invalidating another Lesbian?

195

Do we change partners now instead of dress styles? Do we turn our former ring-around-the-collar scrutiny on our partners now, applying softeners, whiteners and brighteners, starch, stain-remover, anti-static products to reduce clinging in our relationships? Do we redecorate our sexual behaviors every other year, just to keep from getting bored? Are we swapping sexual recipes all the time, so our partner won't get tired of the same menu?

If something needs constant "fixing," maybe we should consider turning our attention elsewhere and giving our energy to issues that will provide us with real momentum and achievement.

Fathers

> "Do you know—I think I should have liked you very much—as a casual acquaintance.
> Yours truly, C. A. Perkins."
>
> —Charlotte Perkins Gilman

This was from a letter Charlotte Perkins Gilman wrote to her father on her twenty-first birthday. Her father had abandoned Charlotte's mother early in the marriage, leaving her with two infants and no way to earn a living.

Patriarchy would make fatherhood appear to be analogous to motherhood: the woman is the mother; the man is the father; both are parents. The reality is very, very different— as incest statistics and unpaid child support illustrate.

The mother carries the fetus for nine months, literally sharing a life-support system with the baby. Frequently she nurses the baby at her own breast, continuing the sharing of her body. Most often, she becomes the primary care-giver. Biological motherhood involves a tremendous investment in time and physical resources. Biological fatherhood requires an ejaculation.

Patriarchy created the institution of fatherhood and marriage to insure male ownership of children, because, in fact, women have babies, not men. Ownership of children would enable a man to exploit them by hiring them out, making them domestic or sexual slaves, or arranging marriages for them that would extend his empire or enhance his social prestige. As "fathers," men could indulge themselves in a sense of immortality through passing property on to a male heir created in their own image.

Fatherhood was never intended to mean that a man would get up at night to feed an infant, that he would have to rearrange his career to meet the demands of child care, or that he would continue to support "his" children after he had lost interest in the mother.

Some feminists are desperately invested in making fatherhood morally, and not just legally, analogous to motherhood. They want men to become accountable, to become nurturing, to cherish the life that they supposedly share responsibility for bringing into the world.

We are talking about the species that invented war, that indulges in pornography, that sees to it that one third of the little girls in this country are raped before they are eighteen—and usually by a "father" figure! Do we really want to push for more men having more access to our children? What if we consider redefining the terms for the nuclear family? What if there are only mothers and children in the world. Men can choose by their actions to become a nurturant "mother", or to remain a self-centered "child."

Let's get rid of a category, fatherhood, that gives men the access of a mother, but that allows them to retain the destructive narcissism of a child.

Anger

Anger is natural in children, but under patriarchy—and especially if the abuse has been early and severe—little girls learn to repress this emotion, or misdirect it toward themselves.

Most women must reclaim our anger. We must go back and find out where we left it. We must remember. It is the hardest work we can do.

Anger is dangerous, because anger is contagious and it always brings change. Anger brings swift repercussions—and often for others who are not associated with the anger. How many wives and daughters have learned that their anger may trigger an episode of violence from the patriarch that will expose other family members or animals to danger? How many of us have learned that confronting an abusive situation at work will put every woman who witnessed the confrontation at risk?

What shall we do with our anger when we are still living in patriarchy? It will make us uncomfortable; it will require that we confront situations in which we have little leverage; it will alienate us from other women. Anger is expensive. Anger may even seem like a luxury.

The obvious answer would be, "Let sleeping dogs lie." But that is precisely what women have been doing for thousands of years, and that is precisely why the world is what it is. *Nothing* changes in patriarchy without anger.

Patriarchy will propagate a number of philosophies that anger is counterproductive, that reasoned arguments and humble petitions are the most powerful tools for social change. It simply isn't so.

Start to notice when you aren't angry and you should be. Go back into your past and figure out when and how you learned not to feel or express anger. Look at your mother, your grandmothers. What did they do with their anger? How was it punished when it did surface? Practice anger. Rehearse it alone. Try it out on friends. What does it sound like? What does it look like? Have compassion on yourself if you do a lot of blurting and retreating when you begin to retrieve it. Anger is a second language.

But press on. And when you have mastered your anger, graduate to rage.

Danger

─────❖─────

"The greatest danger is not being radical enough."

—Mary Daly

In Webster's the first definition of "radical" means "of, relating to, or proceeding from a root." The second definition is "fundamental." It is not until the third definition that "radical" becomes "extreme."

Dictionaries are a wonderful place to clear out one's thinking. Often the later definitions of words have come to mean the opposite of the original definition. It seems that the further along patriarchy progresses, the more corrupt the language becomes.

This is true for "theatre," which originally meant "an outdoor structure for dramatic performances." Later, the definition expanded to "a place of enactment of significant events." This definition, of course, led to the phrase "theater of war," which, to my mind, marks the complete breakdown of the original definition, because now even the wholesale killing of women and children can, by association, be abstracted to a dramatic performance.

Another interesting word is "profession." The first definition is "the act of taking the vows of a religious community." The second definition is "an act of openly declaring or publicly claiming a belief, faith, or opinion." It is not until the fourth definition that we find the meaning most commonly associated with the word today: "a calling requiring specialized knowledge and often long and intensive academic preparation." And as we know, the price of all that specialization and long academic training is frequently the surrender of one's own opinions and beliefs. Too often, membership in a professional class involves a serious erosion of principles and ideals.

"Radical" means going back to the root. Patriarchy grows like a blackberry vine. Taking it on, one branch at a time, is a bloody and ineffectual proposition. Get to the root. Dig deep and get it all out. The whole thing. Don't try to get rid of the racism and leave the classism intact. Don't try to get rid of the homophobia, but leave the woman-hating practices intact. Don't try to get the men out of your life, but leave the male-identified behaviors in your brain.

The greatest cause for remorse is wastefulness. And failing to work from the root in any endeavor puts one at great risk of wasted effort. Frequently when what we are doing seems the most difficult and meeting with the most opposition, the better strategy is to move to a more, not less, radical position.

Truly radical action is off the visible light spectrum of most folks. This is one of the reasons why Lesbians have historically enjoyed a certain immunity. To even recognize the existence of women-loving women poses such a threat to patriarchy, they choose to pretend we don't exist!

Boundaries and Boundary Raiders

"Give me a girl at an impressionable age, and she is mine for life."

- Muriel Spark

These are the words of Jean Brodie, teacher in a private girls' school, in Muriel's novel, *The Prime of Miss Jean Brodie*.

Jean Brodie was a frustrated woman. Unable or unwilling to live the life she wanted, she chose to focus her energies on creating a cult of worshippers for herself among a group of her students. She undertook to shape the tastes and opinions of the girls, in the name of making them the "crême de la crême" during what she called "the prime" of her life.

The novel is written from the point of view of one of her students, a student who was able to escape at least partially from her control. What she depicts is the devastation caused when a figure of respect and authority deliberately invades the intellectual, emotional, and psychic boundaries of those entrusted to her care. The girls' natural development is seriously disrupted, as they strive to live up to the romantic and unattainable ideals of their beloved mentor. For some, their lives are destroyed.

Miss Brodie had access to the girls, because of her authority as a teacher, but also because of the power of her charisma, and her understanding of the developmental phase of their identities. Her interference in their lives constituted emotional incest. The victims of emotional incest have difficulty discriminating between their identity and the identity of the perpetrator. They often identify the abuser's will or interests with their own. They are set up for major co-dependency later in life—or major controlling behaviors of their own. Or suicide.

Not just girls are susceptible to this kind of manipulation. I would amend the quotation to read, "Give me any part of a woman that is developmentally immature, and that part will be mine forever." (Although "mine forever" refers to Miss Brodie's delusional grandeur, none of the girls could escape the permanent imprint of their teacher's interference.)

The point is, many of us have areas of vulnerability—areas where we still have imperfectly formed defenses or incomplete identities. For some of us, it's in the area of sexuality. For others, it's in the area of forming a philosophy of life or a political analysis of our experiences. Many women lack a strong sense of our own appearance or attractiveness.

And, like Miss Brodie, a woman with an agenda can hone in on those of us with these weaknesses and make us "theirs forever."

As radical feminists we are our sisters' keepers. We have a radical obligation to ourselves and to other women to *learn boundaries* and to honor them. We have an obligation to know when we are being violated, and we have an obligation not to take advantage of a woman with poor boundaries.

We have all learned that "no means no," but in patriarchy where women have been so brainwashed, "yes" does not always mean "yes."

Separatism

"Someone once wrote, 'Men are the missing link.' I believe they are too, the link between evil and good. Which is not to say that womyn are not capable of doing bad things. But if womyn were as evil as men, the species would have come to an end long ago, so no one with that malevolent strain in them would have continued to breed the seeds of its destruction.

So where does that leave womyn in general and the Black Lesbian in particular? It leaves us all in one hell of a fix. A fix we will never even remotely begin to cope with so long as we continue to deny the very existence of the evil that surrounds us."

—Anita Cornwell

These are the words of Anita Cornwell, one of the first African American Lesbian writers to publicly adopt a separatist stance.

The Combahee River Collective was an African American feminist group in Boston, and they repudiated Lesbian separatism in the "Combahee River Collective Statement," first published in 1979:

"Although we are feminists and Lesbians, we feel solidarity with progressive Black men and do not advocate the fractionalization that white women who are separatists demand. Our situation as Black people necessitates that we have solidarity around the fact of race, which white women of course do not need to have with white men, unless it is their negative solidarity as racial oppressors. We struggle together with

Black men against racism, while we also struggle with Black men about sexism."

White separatists have been at risk for harboring racism in a political movement that precludes coalition with any men of color. Some white Lesbian separatists—like white feminists—have been dismissive of the struggle against racism by women of color. African American women have excellent reasons to distrust white women's motives in a movement that dismisses an entire segment of their population. On the other hand, Lesbian separatists of all colors have excellent reasons for distrusting the motives of any women in coalition with men, as Lesbian invisibility or outright homophobia have been the traditional order of the day in these organizations.

Coalition and separatism are both strategies, and as such, they both have advantages and drawbacks.

Separatism, whether racial or Lesbian, creates pressure that drives bigots (racists *and* sexists) into coalitions with more politically moderate activists, and coalition can also bring racism and sexism to the surface and impel separatist spin-offs with more focused agendas. I believe that both strategies are viable, depending on one's goals, and can function synergistically. Women can and should be able to move fluidly from one strategy to another, depending upon the field in which they are currently working, the stage of their individual political process, their geographic location, and so forth.

The problem, as I see it, is the problem of trust. Can Lesbian separatists come to a place of trusting that women in coalition will not allow our issues to be homophobically sidelined? Can women in coalition with men come to trust that Lesbian separatists are not indulging in racially exclusive agendas? Can we listen to one another, can we be responsive, and can we learn to value the benefits of both strategies?

Control

<hr>

"I have learned that when I believed myself to be most 'in control' of my mind, my body, my life, I was least 'in control.' When I would have declared, and believed, that I was 'on top' of relationships and events in my life, I was most the victim of my past and the consequences of my experiences. Realizing this in my own life, I have come to believe that the most damaging idea we've learned from our culture is the equation of power with control, and its corollary, the identification of control with autonomy and independence."

—Julia Penelope

These are the words of Lesbian philosopher Julia Penelope, whose writings on Lesbianism have been on the cutting edge for twenty years, and whose writings, to my mind, will remain on that edge for many years to come.

This excerpt is taken from an essay of hers describing her experience as a "stone butch," that is, a Lesbian who makes love to other women, but who does not allow herself to be made love to. Julia has documented her courageous and painful journey toward a different identity, and in her analysis of this process, she strikes deep at the core philosophy of patriarchy.

If control is not autonomy or independence, what is? I maintain it is integrity, which describes a wholeness of being, an integration of perception and experience. And that integration includes a rigorous critique of the conditioning that may have shaped or be shaping one's perceptions and experiences. It is about a way of being, not doing — and yet it does not preclude activism.

Control is about monitoring and manipulating environments and individuals in order to prop up a shaky sense of one's self. Integrity is about knowing who you are, knowing exactly where the boundaries are for your integrity, and knowing how to defend them. In other words, it's about walking your own fences instead of waging perpetual war against your neighbor's cows.

Do We Hear?

—————————

"among my people
it is rude
to listen to another
without making noises
of acknowledgment..."
"... i am a black woman. i am a lesbian.
now make noise
of acknowledgment."

These are excerpts from a poem entitled "Show You Hear," by Terri Lynn Jewell, an African American Lesbian poet and writer. In November 1995, at the age of 41, Terri died of a self-inflicted gunshot wound.

Let us show that we hear by a renewed commitment to anti-racism in predominantly white Lesbian communities and organizations. Let us show we hear by a renewed commitment to confronting homophobia in predominantly heterosexual communities and organizations.

Let us do the work of affirmative action and quota-counting. Let us be accountable to one another. Let us show one another that we are listening. And let us show that we hear.

Acknowledgements

The author and the publisher would like to thank the following for permission to reproduce material used in these essays:

Excerpt from *Black Lesbian in White America* by Anita Cornwell, Naiad Press, 1983, is reprinted with the permission of the author and the publisher.

Excerpt from "Life in the Passing Lane: Exposing the Class Closet" in *Too Queer* by Victoria A. Brownworth, Firebrand Books, Ithaca, NY. Copyright © 1996 by Victoria A. Brownworth, reprinted with the publisher's permission.

Excerpt from *The Women's Spirituality Book* by Diane Stein, Llewellyn Publications, St. Paul, MN, 1987. Reprinted with the publisher's permission.

Excerpts from *Three Guineas* by Virginia Woolf, copyright © 1938 by Harcourt Brace and Company and renewed 1966 by Leonard Woolf, reprinted by permission of the publisher.

Excerpt from *A Room of One's Own* by Virginia Woolf, copyright © 1929 by Harcourt Brace and Company and renewed 1957 by Leonard Woolf, reprinted by permission of the publisher.

Excerpts from "Professions for Women" in *The Death of the Moth and Other Essays* by Virginia Woolf, copyright © 1942 by Harcourt Brace and Company and renewed 1970 by Marjorie T. Parsons, Executrix, reprinted by permission of the publisher.

Excerpt from *The Member of the Wedding*. Copyright © 1946 by Carson McCullers, copyright renewed 1974 by Floria V. Lasky. Reprinted by permission of Houghton Mifflin Co. All rights reserved.

Acknowledgements

Excerpt from "The Brightening Fire," copyright © 1991 by Lynne Yamaguchi Fletcher. Reprinted from *She Who Was Lost is Remembered: Healing from Incest Through Creativity*, edited by Louise M. Wisechild, Seal Press, Seattle, with the publisher's permission.

Excerpt from "Incest - 'Show and Tell,'" copyright © 1991 by Bonnie Martinez. Reprinted from *She Who Was Lost is Remembered: Healing from Incest Through Creativity*, edited by Louise M. Wisechild, Seal Press, Seattle, with the publisher's permission.

Excerpt taken from Laadan, a language constructed by Suzette Haden Elgin for her science fiction novel series, *Native Tongue*. Reprinted with the author's permission.

Excerpt from *Sappho: A Translation by Mary Barnard*, Shambala Publications, Boston. Copyright © 1958 by the Regents of the University of California. Reprinted with the permission of the University of California Press.

Excerpts from *Crusade for Justice: The Autobiography of Ida B. Wells* by Ida B. Wells-Barnett, The University of Chicago Press, Chicago, 1970. Reprinted with the publisher's permission.

Excerpt from *Woman at Point Zero* by Nawal El Saadawi, Zed Books, London, 1983. Reprinted with publisher's permission.

Excerpt from conversation with Jean Mountaingrove of Sunny Valley, Oregon. Reprinted with Jean's permission.

Excerpt from *Not Vanishing*, Press Gang, Vancouver, BC, 1988, from the poem entitled "I Am Not Your Princess" by Chrystos. Reprinted with the author's permission.

Excerpt from *Cassatt and Her Circle: Selected Letters* by Mary Cassatt, edited by Nancy Mowell Matthews, Abbeville Publishing Group, NY, 1984. Reprinted with the publisher's permission.

permission. Button list can be ordered from PO Box 2085, Rancho Cordova, CA 95741-2085. Please include a SASE and $1 for handling.

Excerpt from *Courage* by Amelia Earhart, 1927.

Excerpt from *Willa Cather: A Literary Life* by James Woodress, published by the University of Nebraska Press, Lincoln, NE. Reprinted with the publisher's permission.

Excerpts from *Sula* by Toni Morrison, Plume/Penguin, NY, 1973. Copyright ©1973 by Toni Morrison. Permission granted by International Creative Management, Inc.

Excerpt from *Halfbreed* by Maria Campbell, published by the University of Nebraska Press, Lincoln, NE. Reprinted with the publisher's permission.

Excerpt from *I Know Why the Caged Bird Sings* by Maya Angelou, Random House, NY. Copyright © 1969 by Maya Angelou. Reprinted with the publisher's permission.

Excerpt from "Walking Our Boundaries," from *The Black Unicorn* by Andre Lorde. Copyright © 1978 by Audre Lorde. Reprinted with permission of W.W. Norton & Co., Inc, NY.

Excerpt from *A Raisin in the Sun: The Unfilmed Original Screenplay* by Lorraine Hansberry, Random House, NY, 1992. Screenplay copyright © 1992 Columbia Pictures Industries Inc. Reprinted with the publisher's permission.

Excerpt by Olive Schreiner from *Daughters of Decadence: Women Writers of the Fin de Siecle*, edited by Elaine Showalter, Rutgers University Press, New Brunswick, NJ. Reprinted with the publisher's permission.

Excerpt by Shirley Chisholm from a speech given June 4, 1972.

Acknowledgements

Excerpts from *The Living of Charlotte Perkins Gilman* by Charlotte Perkins Gilman. Introduction by Ann J. Lane. Copyright © 1935, 1963, 1990. The University of Wisconsin Press, Madison, WI. Reprinted with the publisher's permission.

Excerpt from "The Transformation of Silence Into Language and Action," from *Sister Outsider* by Audre Lorde 1984. The Crossing Press, Freedom, CA. Reprinted with the publisher's permission.

Excerpt from *Kiss Hollywood Goodby* by Anita Loos. Copyright © 1974 Anita Loos. Reprinted with permission from Ray Pierre Corsini for the Anita Loos Trust.

Excerpt by Maya Lin from *Lives of Notable Asian Americans: Arts/ Entertainment/ Sports* by Geraldine Gan, Chelsea House, Broomall, PA. Reprinted with the publisher's permission.

Excerpt by Mountain Wolf Woman from *Mountain Wolf Woman: Sister of Crashing Thunder: The Autobiography of a Winnebago Indian*, edited by Lurie, The University of Michigan Press, Ann Arbor, MI, 1961. Reprinted with the publisher's permission.

Excerpt from *Our Voices, Our Lives* by Margaret Randall, Common Courage Press, Monroe, ME. Reprinted with the publisher's permission.

Excerpt from *Patriarchy: Notes from an Expert Witness* by Phyllis Chesler, Common Courage Press, Monroe, ME, 1994. Reprinted with the author's and publisher's permission.

Excerpt by Sara Orne Jewett from "Miss Jewett" in *Not Under Forty* by Willa Cather. Copyright © 1936 Willa Cather. Alfred A. Knopf, Inc., NY. Reprinted with the publisher's permission.

Excerpt by Christabel Pankhurst from *Shoulder to*

ing by Scarecrow Press, Lanthan, MD, 1997. Reprinted with the author's permission.

Excerpt from "Whose Past Are We Reclaiming?" in *Call Me Lesbian* by Julia Penelope, Crossing Press, Freedom, CA, 1992. Reprinted with the author's permission.

Excerpts from "Show You Hear" by Terri Lynn Jewell. Reprinted by permission of Stephanie Byrd.

Excerpt from *The Prime of Miss Jean Brodie* by Muriel Spark. Copyright © 1961 by Muriel Spark. Copyright renewed. Reprinted by permission of HarperCollins Publishers, Inc.

Excerpt from "A Black Feminist Statement" by the Combahee River Collective in *This Bridge Called My Back: Writings by Radical Women of Color*, copyright © 1983 by Cherríe Moraga and Gloria Anzaldúa, editors. Reprinted with permission of the author and of Kitchen Table: Women of Color Press, P.O. Box 40-4920, Brooklyn, NY 11240-4920.

We thank Andrea Dworkin for permission to quote from her published work:

Excerpt from "Trapped in a Pattern of Pain Where No One Can Help," *LA Times*, June 26, 1994.

Excerpt from *Mercy*, Four Walls Eight Windows, NY, 1991.

Excerpt from "The Making of a Radical Feminist," *On the Issues*, Vol. IX, 1988.

Excerpt attributed to Dorothea Dix, July 17, 1887.

Excerpt by Harriet Martineau from "Women," *Society in America*, Vol. III, 1837.

Excerpt attributed to Belva Lockwood, *Outstanding American Women* by Julia F. Lieser, Youth Publications, The Saturday Evening Post Company, Indianapolis, IN, 1977.

Excerpt by Emily Dickinson, #44, St. 1, 1862.

Excerpts by Harriet Tubman from *Scenes in the Life of Harriet Tubman* by Sarah H. Bradford, originally published in 1869, republished Peter Smith, Gloucester, MA, 1981.

Excerpt from *Middlemarch* by George Eliot, 1871-72.

Excerpts from *Wuthering Heights* by Emily Bronte, 1847.

Excerpt from *Science and Health with Key to the Scriptures* by Mary Baker Eddy, 1875.

Excerpt from *Woman, Church, and State* by Matilda Joslyn Gage, Persephone Press, Watertown, MA, 1980. Originally published in 1893.

Excerpt from the Seneca Falls Resolutions, NY, 1848.

Excerpt from *Lelia* by George Sand, Vol. I, 1833.

Excerpt by Donaldina Cameron from *Chinatown's Angry Angel* by Mildred Crowl Martin, Pacific Books, Palo Alto, CA, 1977.

Excerpt from *Harriet Martineau's Autobiography*, Vol. I, 1877.

Excerpt from Lillian Hellman's letter to the House Committee on Un-American Activities, May 19, 1952. Cited in *Bartlett's Familiar Quotations*, Little, Brown, and Company, Boston, 1980.

Excerpt from *Cranford* by Elizabeth Gaskell, 1853.

Excerpt from *Letters from New York,* Vol. II, by Lydia Maria Child, December 31, 1845.

Excerpt by Eleanora Duse quoted by Louis Schneider in *Le Gaulois*, July 27, 1922.

Excerpt by Eleanora Duse from *Vita de Arrigo Boito* by Piero Nordi, 1942.

Acknowledgements

Excerpt by Clara Lee from an article in *The San Francisco Chronicle*, February 8, 1914, p.3.

Malgasy proverb from *The Black Woman's Gumbo Ya-Ya: Quotations by Black Women* edited by Terri L. Jewell, The Crossing Press, Freedom, CA, 1993.

Excerpt from "Whose Past Are We Reclaiming?" in *Call Me Lesbian* by Julia Penelope, Crossing Press, Freedom, CA, 1992. Reprinted with the author's permission.

Excerpts from "Show You Hear" by Terri Lynn Jewell. Reprinted by permission of Stephanie Byrd.

Excerpt from *The Prime of Miss Jean Brodie* by Muriel Spark. Copyright © 1961 by Muriel Spark. Copyright renewed. Reprinted by permission of HarperCollins Publishers, Inc.

Excerpt from "A Black Feminist Statement" by the Combahee River Collective in *This Bridge Called My Back: Writings by Radical Women of Color*, copyright © 1983 by Cherrie Moraga and Gloria Anzaldua, editors. Reprinted with permisson of the author and of Kitchen Table: Women of Color Press, PO Box 40-4920, Brooklyn, NY 11240-4920.

Index

About the Author

CAROLYN GAGE is a Lesbian-feminist playwright, activist, and director. Her collection of plays, *The Second Coming of Joan of Arc and Other Plays* (HerBooks, Santa Cruz, CA, 1994), was named National Finalist for the 1995 Lambda Literary Award in drama. In 1996, her musical *The Amazon All-Stars* was the title play for an anthology of Lesbian plays by Applause Books. She has written the first book on Lesbian theatre production, *Take Stage! How to Direct and Produce a Lesbian Play* (Scarecrow Press, 1997), as well as *Scenes and Monologues for Lesbian Actors,* another first. Gage has been the recipient of the Arch and Bruce Brown Foundation Award, the Nancy Dean Distinguished Playwriting Award, the Oregon Playwrights Award, the Lesbian Theatre Conference Distinguished Playwriting Award and grants from the Oregon Institute of Literary Arts, and the Oregon Arts Council.